A SHORT HISTORY OF JAPANESE ARCHITECTURE

Gates of Daimyo mansions in Edo.
(From the *Tōtō Meisho* of Hiroshige.)

A Short History of Japanese Architecture

by A. L. SADLER, M.A.

CHARLES E. TUTTLE COMPANY

Rutland, Vermont & Tokyo, Japan

European Representatives
Continent: BOXERBOOKS, INC., Zurich
British Isles: PRENTICE-HALL INTERNATIONAL, INC., London

Published by the Charles E. Tuttle Company,
of Rutland, Vermont & Tokyo, Japan
with editorial offices at
15 Edogawa-cho, Bunkyo-ku, Tokyo, Japan
© 1962 by Charles E. Tuttle Co.

Library of Congress Catalog Card No. 62-21539

1st edition published 1941 by Angus and Robertson, Limited Sydney
and London through a grant from the Carnegie Corporation of New York
1st Tuttle edition, 1963

PRINTED IN JAPAN

Yo ni furu wa
Sara ni shigure no
Yadori ka na.
Truly man's living in this world
Is but a shelter from a shower.

Tzu Hsia, the disciple of Confucius, said: "The inferior man always embellishes his mistakes."

PREFACE

IT was probably an attraction to Japanese buildings and gardens, first acquired from a perusal of Morse's *Japanese Homes and their Surroundings* in the Bodleian Library many years ago, as much as the historical interest or the wise counsel of that very eminent orientalist Dr C. J. Ball, that decided me to go to Japan rather than to the Near East, which was then the more obvious region for research. And these houses and gardens were certainly no disappointment, but a source of continual pleasure all the time I stayed there—a diversion I regret I have missed since leaving Japan, for Australia is in these things the diametric opposite to that country as it is in most others.

And though a layman in architectural matters, with only a claim to some appreciation of them as a student of history, I have lived for some ten years or so in three old Japanese houses in an ancient castle town, as well as built a new one. Perhaps there may, in this, be an application of the Japanese proverb which states that the acolyte before the temple gate repeats the scriptures he has not learned, or, as one adroit translator puts it, "The saint's maid quotes Latin." Moreover, fortunate residence in a comely old English town and six years of leisure in one of the most elegant of Oxford colleges, both in buildings and garden, were a natural education in what is shapely and harmonious in various types of Western architecture. So it has been an entertaining task after many days to gather these drawings and plans from the books I happen to have read, and put them together in some sort of chronological order in the hope that they may be a direct visual means of giving some insight into the phases through which Japanese culture has passed and the elements of which it is composed.

A. L. SADLER.

Sydney,
July, 1941

CONTENTS

CHAPTER   PAGE

  I. INTRODUCTION - - - - - - - - - - 1

 II. EARLY PERIOD (660 B.C.-A.D. 540) - - - - - - 8

 III. THE INTRODUCTION OF BUDDHISM. ASUKA PERIOD (540-640) 15

 IV. HAKUHŌ PERIOD (640-720) - - - - - - - 20

 V. TEMPYO PERIOD (720-780) - - - - - - - 22

 VI. HEIAN PERIOD (780-1190) - - - - - - - 27

 VII. KAMAKURA PERIOD (1190-1340) - - - - - - 39

VIII. MUROMACHI PERIOD (1340-1570) - - - - - - 47

 IX. MOMOYAMA PERIOD (1570-1616) - - - - - - 54

 X. EDO PERIOD (1616-1860) - - - - - - - 67

 XI. THE SHOGUN'S RECEPTION OF THE EMPEROR - - - 85

 XII. BUILDING REGULATIONS IN THE TOKUGAWA PERIOD - - 87

XIII. SHŌJI, FUSUMA AND CEILINGS - - - - - - 90

XIV. PRIVY AND BATHROOM - - - - - - - - 93

 XV. THE KITCHEN - - - - - - - - - 99

XVI. THE ARCHITECT - - - - - - - - - 99

   APPENDIXES - - - - - - - - - 105

   BIBLIOGRAPHY - - - - - - - - 129

   INDEX - - - - - - - - - - 135

   PLATES - - - - - - - - - - 141

ILLUSTRATIONS

PLATE

Gates of Daimyo mansions in Edo. *Frontispiece*

1. Forms of ancient houses.
2. FIG. 1. Plan of Izumo shrine. FIG. 2. Plan of Otori shrine. FIG. 3. Plan of Sumiyoshi shrine. FIG. 4. Umbrella shape plan of early house. FIG. 5. Conjectured most ancient form of house called Tenchi Kongen Miya-zukuri. FIG. 6. The Great Shrine of Izumo.
3. FIG. I. The Ise Daijingu or Main Shrine at Ise. FIG. 2. Ordinary Shimmei style shrine.
4. The Sumiyoshi shrine.
5. FIG. 1. Kokuchu Sumái house in Iga district of Shiga prefecture. FIG. 2. Old house in Amatsu village. FIG. 3. House at Shirakawa, Hida province.
6. FIG. 1. House in Tansei village. FIG. 2. Old house in Iwakura village.
7. Sites of the ancient capitals in Yamato.
8. The capital of Asuka. Imperial mausolea.
9. Pillars of Asuka, Haku-ho, Tempyo, and Konin eras (590-824 A.D.).
10. Pillars of Fujiwara and Kamakura periods (824-1392 A.D.).
11. Pillars of Muromachi, Momoyama and Edo periods (1392-1868).
12. Elbow brackets (single, double and triple).
13. Elbow brackets (sextuple, quintuple, septuple, groups of three, and close grouping).
14. Frog-crotches of Asuka, Heian, Muromachi and Momoyama periods.
15. FIG. 1. Tail rafter bracket-supports, Kamakura period. FIGS 2-5. King-post construction of Kamakura and later periods.
15A. FIG.1. Relic casket in the shape of a tope from Manikyala, first century A.D. FIG. 2. Bracket capital of the fifth century at Nassick. FIG. 3. Pillar and capital of the fifth century at Ajanta. FIG. 4. Lotus and water-pot capital of India. FIG. 5. Palace façade at Barhut, showing pipal leaf window arches. FIG. 6. Bracket and strut construction of eleventh century at Mount Abu. FIG. 7. Nepalese Dagoba. FIG. 8. Wooden Jaina temple at Canara.
16. FIG. 1. Professor Amanuma's restoration of the Kondo of the Hōryuji. FIG. 2. Section of the cloister gallery of the Hōryuji.
17. The Kondo of the Hōryuji, elevation and section.
18. The five-storied pagoda of the Hōryuji.
19. Elbow brackets of the earliest period. Hōryuji temple, seventh century.
20. FIG. 1. Kudara style, Hōryuji type. FIG. 2. Kudara style, Shitennōji type. FIG. 3. Kara style (Nara), T'ang. FIG. 4. Zen style (Kamakura), Sung.
21. The capital of Heijo at Nara.
22. Pagoda of the Yakushiji temple.
23. FIGS 1 and 2. Three-branch bracketing of the pagoda of the Yakushiji. FIG. 3. Pierced iron "spray" of the pinnacle of the Yakushiji pagoda. FIG. 4. Large and small capitals of the bracketing of the above.
24. FIG. 1. Plan of the Hōryuji temple. FIG. 2. Plan of the Tōdaiji temple as it was in the Tempyo era (729-748).
25. The Toshōdaiji. Kondo, section, detail of bracketing and side view.
26. Yume-dono of the Hōryuji temple, with its water-pot pinnacle.
27. The Imperial Storehouse of the Tōdaiji, called Shōsōin.
28. FIG. 1. Professor Amanuma's restoration of the seven-story pagoda of the Tōdaiji. FIG. 2. Hokkedo of the Tōdaiji.

29. The Heian capital. Plan showing the location of the Imperial City, the Palace, the Hōraku-in, the Hassho-in, the University, the Shinsen-en park, the markets, the Saiji and the Toji.

30. The Heian capital. Figs 1-3. Lay-outs of blocks of thirty-two rows. Fig. 4. Lay-out of the eastern market. Fig. 5. The Shishinden or throne hall with the Nan-en or southern court in front of it.

31. The Heian capital. The Dai-Dairi or Imperial City with the palace, the Hasshōin and Hōgakuin halls of ceremony, the eight departments of State and the various palace and government offices. Kōnin period (810-824).

32. The Heian capital. Imperial palace (plan).

33. The Heian capital. The Chōdōin or Hasshōin, and the Hōgakuin, within the Imperial City.

34. The Heian capital. The plan of the Seiryōden of the palace.

35. Fig. 1. Nobleman's mansion of the Fujiwara age in Shinden style. Fig. 2. Plan of Shinden style mansion.

36. Fig. 1. Plan of the Kanin palace. Fig. 2. Plan of Shinden style mansion.

37. Streets in the capital of Heian.

38. Phoenix Hall (Hōō-do) of the Byōdōin at Uji. Plan, triple bracketing, hand-rail and pendant of gable.

39. Hall of the Fukiji temple in Bungo, Kyushu. Elevation and section.

40. The Hakusui Amida-do, Uchigo village, Iwaki district, Fukushima province. Elevation and section. Built in 1160.

41. Reconstruction of the city of Hiraizumi after Sato.

42. The Konjikido of the Chusonji.

43. Five-story pagoda of the Daigōji, showing breadths and heights of roofs.

44. Five-story pagoda of the Daigōji with geometrical proportions, after the diagram of Professor Amanuma.

45. The Hachiman shrine at Usa, and the Hiyoshi shrine at Hieizan.

46. The Kamo shrine, Kyoto, side and front views. Rebuilt in 1863. Edo period.

47. Professor Amanuma's restoration of the Yugi pagoda of Mount Koya.

48. Kamakura, with Shogun's mansion inset, after Sato.

49. Mansion of the governor of the Eastern Provinces (Kanto-Kanryo) at Kamakura in the Muromachi period.

50. A birth. Showing interior of a mansion, Kamakura period.

51. The Shōin of a monastery.

52. Fig. 1. Wall and gate with guard-house over it, in military residence of Kamakura period. Fig. 2. Bell-tower of the Tōdaiji, Nara, side view elevation and section, front view half-section.

53. The three-story pagoda of the Kōfukuji, Nara. Early Kamakura style.

54. Stupa-shaped pagoda of Ishiyama temple. Built by Minamoto Yoritomo.

55. The Nandaimon of the Tōdaiji.

56. Details of the Kanshinji.

57. The Shariden of the Engakuji, Kamakura.

58. Fig. 1. Renge gate of the Toji Temple, Kyoto. Fig. 2. Details of roof construction of the Kamakura period. Kozanji temple, Chofu, Yamaguchi prefecture.

59. The Sutra library (Kyōzō) at Kami Daigo temple.

60. Fig. 1. Kanshinji temple, side view. Fig. 2. The Kaisando or Founder's Hall of the Eihōji, Toyooka village, Gefu prefecture (Kamakura period).

61. The octagonal pagoda of the Anrakuji temple at Bessho village, Chiisagata district, province of Nagano.

62. The Great Pagoda (Daito) of Negoro temple. Elevation and section.

Illustrations

63. Ginkakuji, Kyoto. Front view and side view.
64. Details of the Kinkakuji.
65. Fig. 1. Side view of the Kibitsu shrine, Ichinomiya, Okayama prefecture, built in 1390. Figs 1 to 10. Decorated beam-ends from the bell-tower of the Tōdaiji, Nara.
66. Fig. 1. Oshi-ita. Fig. 2. Early form of *shōji*, called Konmeichi *shōji*.
67. Plan of Azuchi castle and surroundings.
68. Fig. 1. Plans of Osaka castle. Fig. 2. Old sketch of fortified field headquarters about 1600. Fig. 3. Rampart of Osaka castle. Fig. 4. Gate of the castle of Sakura. Fig. 5. Castle Gate (Masugata).
69. Osaka castle as defended by Hideyori in 1614.
70. Fig. 1. Kitchen and refectory of the Myōhōin Kyoto; side view and front view. Fig. 2. The eight-fold roof of the Momoyama period.
71. Dai-butsu-den or hall of the Great Buddha of the Tōdaiji, Nara.
72. Fig. 1. The Great Buddha temple of the Hōkōji, from a picture of 1794. Fig. 2. The Hiunkaku of the Nishi Hongwanji from the western side.
73. The Kokakudai bathroom of the Hiunkaku.
74. The Hiunkaku villa.
75. Jinya or official residence of a smaller feudal lord or local official.
76. The castle and town of Fukuoka, built and laid out by Kuroda Josui and his son Nagamasa after 1600.
77. Plan of the Hon Maru of the Castle of Fukuoka.
78. Plan of the castle town of Matsue.
79. Fig. 1. Plan of the Hon Maru of Okayama castle. Fig. 2. The mansion of the Hon Maru of Okayama castle in the time of Ikeda Mitsumasa, 1632-1672.
80. Plan of the castle town of Okayama.
81. Fig. 1. Plan of the moated castle town of Okayama, Bizen. Fig. 2. Plan of the Clan College (Han Gakko) at Okayama.
82. Plan of the castle town of Takada in Echigo.
83. Plan of the city Nagasaki.
84. Fig. 1. Keep of the castle of Nagoya. Fig. 2. Keep of Matsue (1600).
85. Fig. 1. Keep of Okayama castle (1597). Fig. 2. Keep of Inuyama castle (1600) Fig. 3. Keep of Kumamoto castle (1596). Fig. 4. Keep of the castle of Matsumoto in Shinano (1590).
86. Fig. 1. The original keep of Edo castle. Fig. 2. Flanking guardhouse at entrance of Edo castle.
87. Village of craftsmen laid out by Honami Kōetsu at Takagamine.
88. General plan of Edo castle.
89. Edo castle. O Omote or Outer Palace of the Hon Maru.
90. Edo castle. O Oku or Inner Palace of the Hon Maru, plan 1.
91. Edo castle. O Oku or Inner Palace of the Hon Maru, plan 2.
92. Plan of the mansion of a court noble.
93. Gates of Daimyos' mansions in Edo.
94. Fig. 1. Plan of the Tōshōgu shrine at Nikko. Fig. 2. Plan of Nijo castle.
95. Upper section of the five-storied pagoda at Nikko.
96. Lower section of the five-storied pagoda at Nikko.
97. Plan of the Zen temple of Myōshinji, and plan of its kitchen and refectory.
98. Plan of Zen temple of Manpukuji.
99. Imperial Palace, Kyoto. Koka gate and Seiryōden.
100. Imperial Palace, Kyoto. Front gate and Shishinden.
101. The Imperial Palace shrine or Kashiko-dokoro.
102. Fig. 1. Front of a theatre. Fig. 2. The theatre quarter of Saru-waka-cho.

103. Plan of the Yoshiwara pleasure quarter in Edo.
104. FIG. 1. Side street in Edo with guard-house and gates for closing the thoroughfare. FIG. 2. Fireman's watch-tower. FIG. 3. Fireproof storehouse.
105. FIG. 1. Plan of public bath house at Osaka. FIG. 2. Plan of public bath house in Edo. FIG. 3. Bath tub with gabled porch in public bath house.
106. Bathroom interior.
107. FIG. 1. Large farm-house in Tsutsuki village, Kyoto. FIG. 2. Narrow residence characteristic of Kyoto, known as "eel housing".
108. Korean peasant's house built of logs and mud.
109. Kachu-yashiki or Samurai residence at Kita-bori, Matsue.
110. FIG. 1. Plan of the residence of a Samurai of middle class. FIG. 2. Street front and gatehouse of the above.
111. A Benie print-seller.
112. FIG. 1. Privy of an inn at the end of a short covered way at right angles to a veranda. FIG. 2. The interior of above, with ventilation window.
113. Tiles.
114. Roof shapes.
115. Lattice windows.
116. Stair-cases.
117. Ceilings.
118. Wooden lanterns.
119. Hot spring bath houses.
120. FIG. 1. The simple staircase of an inn. FIG. 2. A renaissance cupola added to a hot spring bathing hotel in pure Japanese style.
121. Plan and elevation of a modern house in Japanese style.
122. Section of an ordinary Japanese house to show construction.

A SHORT HISTORY OF JAPANESE ARCHITECTURE

CHAPTER I

INTRODUCTION

THE purpose of this work is to give a short account of the growth of Japanese architecture and its connexion with the history and culture of the people. Countries write their history very legibly in the things they build and the way they treat the face of the earth, and the Japanese have done it as clearly as any. The character of the land with its abundance of timber and the natural taste of the inhabitants for this medium have combined to present us with the most advanced wooden architecture in the world; and the isolation of Japan, on the one hand, and its relations with the continent, on the other, have preserved in these islands specimens of architecture that do not survive in the countries of their origin.

The earliest buildings of Japan are the simple rectilinear structures of the primitive dwelling houses which survive only in a somewhat modified form in the Shinto shrines, and seem to be of the same type as those found in the islands of the Pacific. And residences have continued to be predominantly of this type, for it seems to suit the temperament of the people. The severe winter cold prevalent in most parts of the Japanese islands has not caused much modification in what is essentially a sub-tropical style, or even brought about the introduction of any heating system like those found in Korea and China. Simplicity has been preferred to warmth, and the cold kept at bay to a certain extent by braziers and padded garments. But these houses are no more than simple construction, and architecture, properly speaking, entered Japan with Buddhism in the sixth century. The origin of both the philosophy and the architecture was India and they were only modified in passing through China and Korea. From the stone reliefs of the post-Asoka period at Sanchi and elsewhere it is evident that the early Indian buildings were also of wood,[1] for even after they were rendered in stone they retained all the characteristics of their original construction. But in India stone and brick entirely superseded this wooden style and even in China these materials were largely used for temples, bridges, gates and pagodas. In Japan this architecture assumed its original wooden form and did not depart from it, for (with the exception of the stylobates, foundation stones, castle ramparts, and facings of moats and gates in and after the sixteenth century) nothing but Buddhist statuary, garden ornaments and tombstones has ever been made of anything but wood.

The introduction of this Indian style into Japan was not unlike that of classical architecture into England, though there is less variation in it than there is between Romanesque, the different types of Gothic, and the later Renaissance, styles. The principal difference is in the details of the pillars and bracketing and the slope of the roofs. It never affected residences to the same extent either, for the most elaborate mansions in Japan were quite unlike temples. They merely borrowed a little bracketing here and there, and some patterns on the roof tiles. Castles came later, and were not much used as residences; we do not find any such mannered institutions as Hatfield, Blenheim, or Castle Howard, nor anything like the odd Gothic fancies of Pugin, though some comparison might perhaps be made between Knole and the residential part of Edo Castle.

The Japanese love of nature made them disinclined to shut themselves up in a kind of big storehouse even though the winds might blow. That sort of building they reserved for their possessions; and their residences, whether military, civil or ecclesiastical, were never much more than structures just stout enough to keep off the weather, particularly the sun and rain, and especially designed as shelters from which to view the garden or a distant landscape. It is for this latter purpose as a rule that a room is added in the roof; for, with the exception of shops and inns and restaurants and some houses in big cities, most Japanese houses are single-storied, though that does not mean that they are necessarily lacking in height. Important buildings such

---

[1] Ferguson calls attention to the similarities between the wooden architecture of the Himalayan districts of Kashmir and Nepal and the timber buildings of Sweden and Norway, and Professor Strzygowski has developed the subject in his interesting and learned work *Early Church Art in Northern Europe.*

as palaces, temples, and mansions, and even the houses of large land-owners, have very lofty roofs quite high enough to contain several stories, and temples that have a double roof with two sets of eaves one over the other do not use the space in the upper one.

On the whole Japanese buildings give the impression of being planned from within outwards, for use and not to be looked at from outside. As they are so often secluded behind a courtyard the gate is apt to be the most noticeable feature, and, since by its shape it denoted the rank of its owner, it was at times of a somewhat elaborate nature. The great gates of the Imperial Palace, the four-legged gate of the Court noble and the threefold or storied gate of the temple are all significant, and it was not perhaps so strange that in later days the gates of the mansions of the feudal nobility should be regulated by the government according to their owners' incomes.

It is probably well known that one of the ancient titles of the Emperor, *Mikado* means "August Gate," but it may not be generally realized how very architectural are most titles in Japan. The expression translated "His Majesty" (*Heika*) means "below the steps" of the palace), and that translated "Highness" (*Denka*), "below the mansion." *Tono* (mansion) still means "nobleman," while another medieval word *yakata,* with the same significance, is now obsolete. *In* (temple) was the word for a retired Emperor or a dead Shogun. *Mon-in* (Dowager Empress) means the "Retired One of the palace gate." *Kamon* (House Gate) means "descendants of the House," i.e. the Tokugawa family, while the word for lineage itself, *mombatsu,* means "one whose gate is meritorious," and *meimon* (gate of repute) means "a noble family." *Tsubone* (the title of a lady-in-waiting) means "courtyard," and the wives of nobles and Shoguns were called *kita-no-kata* (the lady of the north or inner side of the house), or *mi-daidokoro* (august kitchen), with the same meaning. The terms still in use for a lady, *okusama* or *go reikei*[2] mean respectively "inner apartment" and "august bed-chamber." We have, too, *go bō* (honourable cell) for a monk, and *o heya sama* (honourable chamber) for a noble's concubine. Similar, too, is the use of such words as *-sai* (study) and *-an* (cottage) for the terminations of the literary names of scholars and aesthetes and retired people.

---

[2] These expressions are, like other honorifics, designed to avoid direct reference to the persons concerned.

The material of Japanese buildings is almost exclusively wood with the exception of the pottery of the tiles. All joints are mortised, tenoned and pegged, and the gutters are of wood or bamboo. Until recently there were only bamboo pipes, and water was drawn from a well with wooden buckets and a pulley of porcelain. No nails were used anywhere and the only things likely to be of metal would be the pushes of the sliding doors, and the iron shutters of the windows of the fireproof storehouse if there was one. It is not perhaps surprising that in the technique of wood-working Japanese surpass other nations, for construction is nowhere hidden and the surface of the material is left plain without paint both within and without—the only exception being the lacquering of some details, the preparation for which requires a very exacting standard of cabinet work.

Since Japan has always been autocratically governed and the people have never had any say in the administration, buildings like parliament houses or town or moot halls are conspicuous by their absence until modern times. In fact, places of assembly of any kind except bath houses and theatres are rare, for gatherings of people were not regarded with any favour by the government, and where they existed were always supervised and inspected by it. Even law courts were not very noticeable, because the commissioners for justice, who were both judicial and administrative, dispensed this commodity in their own mansions and in their own fashion. And this fashion did not run so much to prisons and dungeons as did some others, for though the former did exist, the custom of prescribing such penalties as did not require any building, and confining handcuffed in their own houses people who seemed to require such restraint, resulted in very considerable economy. The Shogun, for instance, did not need such a building as the Tower to confine an objectionable nobleman, but ordered him under arrest in the mansion of another baron. If anything further were needed he would be exiled at his own expense or ordered to commit suicide on his own mats.

Buddhist temples, again, are chiefly colleges or monasteries or both, and the congregational element is not prominent in them, while in Shinto shrines it is not present at all, for worship is purely individual and sporadic. As time went on, places of assembly were more and more restricted, till in the Tokugawa era the only places where people could congregate were theatres and pleasure quarters, both supervised, and prohibited for the governing class.

The Japanese residence, being but a succession of rooms without walls and only divided by sliding doors, does not admit of much privacy—a fact that must have had considerable influence on the manners of its inhabitants; for without suitable etiquette and uncommon neatness it would not be tolerable to live in. And it is likely that the comparative abstinence of the Japanese woman from romantic adventures is to no small extent due to her life in a house that is little more than one large room open at any time to a *coup d'oeil* from one end to the other. What chance, asks E. V. Lucas, has cupid in Holland where there are no groves? Much less chance has he in the Japanese house where there are not even walls to have ears. This does not apply so much to the men, whose inclinations in this direction are catered for in many-storied pavilions.

Fire and earthquake have doubtless helped to keep Japanese architecture what it is, for a building out of which the inmates can step at once from any part is convenient for both, while the construction even of quite lofty pagodas has proved fairly stable in the latter.

Fully as important as the building of palace, mansion, temple or residence, if not more so, is the garden, the treatment of the space that surrounds them. Though this is entirely a separate subject it has the closest connexion with architecture, because the garden is usually planned with the buildings, which are arranged about it with a courtyard or semi-courtyard effect, or with detached parts joined by covered ways or bridges. So the garden is not so much an adjunct to the house as an essential part of it, to be designed by an expert together with it or before it. This is why there is greater variety in the houses than might be considered probable when the construction is as standardized as it is, for all rooms have long been multiples of a *tatami* or floor-mat[3] (6 x 3 feet) and all sliding doors are the same height and width (3·8 by 3 feet) with a fixed size for the pillars according to the scale of the

---

[3] The origin of the *tatami* is ascribed to the Empress Jingo who noticed and admired some fine reeds in the province of Bingo when returning from the conquest of Korea. Her attendants wove them into a mat of which Her Majesty also much approved. Ever since Bingo has been famous for its *tatami*. It is significant that the cultivation of the reed there on a large scale is dated from the era Koji (1555), about the time when we hear of floors being wholly covered with these mats.

building. All of which makes for economy and rapidity of construction.

It will be noted, however, that, though the Japanese house seems for some centuries to have been very unlike that of any Western country, as it is traced farther back it becomes less so. The characteristic mats disappear from the floors, and the ceiling from the roof, while small windows[4] take the place of the papered *shōji*, for sliding doors were yet unknown. The thatched roof and earthen floor make it a peasant's hut such as must have been fairly universal in those times. The changes took place in the big cities, where the best artisans and architect-artificers competed for the favour of Shogun or feudal lord —in the Imperial Capital of Kyoto, or the military capitals of Kamakura or Edo, or the great commercial centres like Osaka, Sakai or Nagasaki. But in the remote country conditions do not change much, and the country of Japan is still very isolated between ranges of hills and narrow winding valleys or small islands where even now few but country folk go. So there may still be seen survivals from the pretatami era, dwellings lived in as they have been from the earliest times. And what there is beyond this shows very clearly how the Indian culture, together with sculpture and painting influenced by the Greek colonies of Gandhara, came across by way of China and Korea, sometimes indirectly through the latter country, and in later times more directly from China. For Japan has never been slow in adopting advantages from a dominant country and in showing less enthusiasm for a decadent one.

Japanese architecture is described as a branch of Chinese, but little of the Chinese is indigenous. China is somewhat to Japan as Rome is to England, but behind China lay India, the equivalent of Greece. And India in her turn is perhaps indebted to Persia and Babylonia, as is Greece to Crete and Egypt. Much, therefore, of this Japanese culture may be of Aryan origin, for the influence of Buddhist and Hindu thought shaped the Japanese mind in the same way as Semitic monotheism did that of Europe.

---

[4] In the smaller fourteenth, fifteenth and sixteenth century houses in England there were unglazed windows with oak bars set diagonally, with shutters inside, those of the lower ones sliding in grooves and those of the upper hinged on hooks. (Lloyd's *History of the English House*, pp. 332-3.)

The bell of the Jetavana Vihara
Tolls the knell of the impermanence of phenomena.[5]

But in spite of the Japanese conviction of the impermanence of things, it is remarkable what a large number of interesting and ancient buildings are still to be seen in the country. From the famous Hōryuji monastery of the seventh century right on, these massive wooden structures reveal the characteristics of the various dynasties of China as well as the original inspiration from India. It is no longer possible to see these things in China, for there disintegration and destruction have been fatal to the past; like other continental lands, it has been subject to rough invaders whom not even the "Ten thousand mile long castle" could keep out. Destruction there has been, too, in Japan, and what remains is but a small part of what once was; but in spite of the damage caused by fires and civil wars there has been a great deal of intelligent rebuilding and restoration, which still continues—as witness the recent re-creation of the great keep of Hideyoshi's castle by the city of Osaka exactly as it was, but in steel and concrete. Great hotels and theatres are also being built in this Momoyama style, and even Christian churches are being put up in Japanese style as they were in the sixteenth century, instead of in suburban Gothic as they were formerly in the Meiji era.

Moreover (and I am, of course, indebted to them for everything in this book) there is a large number of eminent professors and scholars in Japan who have investigated and compared and catalogued and repaired their masterpieces of architecture, and published admirable works illustrated by fine photographs that supply a mass of information about them. Professors Ito, Sekino, Kida, Amanuma and Fujita are among the most outstanding of these, and this book is no more than a résumé of what they have written. With a view to increasing its usefulness for those who wish to examine really good and detailed photographs of the structures mentioned, I have added references to Professor Amanuma's great work, *A Pictorial Record of the History of Japanese Architecture* (*Nippon Kenchikushi Zuroku*), indispensable to any really interested in the subject, consisting of a series of illustrations of all the important buildings, accompanied by comments in Japanese. Though the comment may not be understandable the pictures speak for themselves.

---

[5] *Heike Monogatari* I, *i*. The first Buddhist Monastery built on ground belonging to Prince Jeta at Savatthi.

CHAPTER II

EARLY PERIOD (660 B.C.—A.D. 540)

THOUGH no specimens of the most ancient Japanese buildings have survived, their nature can to a large extent be conjectured from descriptions in the ancient writings such as the *Kōjiki* and the *Nihongi,* from pictures and models found in the dolmen tombs, and from the Shinto shrines which conservative sentiment has preserved little changed from the earliest times. It is written that in the days of the Emperor Suinin, who succeeded in 29 B.C., the sacred mirror and regalia were removed from the palace where they had been hitherto, and this act marked the separation of residence and shrine. The shrine, which is that of Ise, was evidently built just like the residence and has not since been altered. The regulation that it should be rebuilt every twenty-five years, i.e., every generation, is no doubt a survival of the custom of moving to a new palace on the death of an Emperor, since birth and death are the greatest pollutions. Parturition houses are spoken of in the ancient texts and are even now still found in some parts of the country.

In the details of its construction the Ise shrine is the earliest type, for its roof is perfectly straight and it is built in the simplest manner without any ornament. The rafters project in the form of a crotch above the roof and the ridge lies in the angle of these crotches, while on that again are short logs to hold it in place. Originally its timbers were bound together with wistaria withes like those of the palace, but later they came to be secured with peg and mortise.

This type of roof was originally forbidden to all but Imperial Residences and the *Kōjiki* mentions the case of the roof of a noble being pulled down because it was too high.[1] And to this day in Japan the height of the roof is a sign of social standing, as it was in the

---

[1] Among the Naga people of the Assam hills it seems these "horns" denote distinction. *Vide* von Führer-Haimendorf's *Naked Nagas.*

Tokugawa period when only farmers of some importance in a village were allowed to have anything above the ordinary one, or such elaborations as a hipped gable or a projecting wing.

The models and carvings that have been excavated show a high pitched roof sometimes of the sort called *irimoya* or hipped gable, and several of these houses are raised above the ground on pillars and entered by a ladder like the Ise shrine. All these early dwellings are very definitely of the Polynesian type, from which the Japanese dwelling house has never departed much; it is only after the entry of Buddhism into Japan that temples began to be built in the Chinese, or more correctly, the Indian, style, for such it really is, and after a while this came to affect the shrine and residence. Tiles and bracketed capitals and ornamental windows made their appearance and the line of the roof assumed a curve. On the other hand, the native style in its turn reacted on this Buddhist architecture in restraining the use of colour and ornament and maintaining a severe line and wooden construction, as contrasted with the extravagant curves and brick and stone structures favoured in China. Though the earlier temples were coloured outside as well as in, with some exceptions[2] shrines remained of unpainted timber. But though the Imperial Shrine of Ise has retained so many early characteristics, in one respect that of Izumo, which commemorates the equally ancient rulers of that province who handed over their dominion to the descendants of the Sun Goddess, has perhaps kept an older style in its plan. Unlike Ise which has the entrance in the front (*hira-iri*) Izumo has it in the gable end (*tsuma-iri*) and the interior is divided into two by a partition extending from the pillar in the centre to the side wall. This shrine is thirty-six feet square without its verandas and has a gabled roof. The entrance is on the right-hand side of the centre, thus recalling that of the primitive hut, like a tent of brushwood, which Japanese archaeologists postulate as the primitive home of the ordinary people in succession to the dug-out which may have been the earliest of all. Thus, should necessity bring Japan back to this condition, as it threatens to do with Europe, it may well be regarded, like conscription, as but a return to the good old times.

This square form is found also in ancient China, and the possibility

---

[2] E.g. those of Inari the Food God. There is an entertaining proverb: "If Inari's shrine fence was not red people would not believe in him."

that there has been some influence from the continent must not be overlooked, in view of the close relations between the Izumo Deities and the mainland. But this shape, too, has always been to a great extent that of the ordinary farm-house in Japan, modified by additions where more room was needed.[3] The space is then divided into four rooms round the central pillar. This pillar (Mi-naka-bashira, the August Central Pillar) seems to be that which Izanami and Izanagi, the Japanese Adam and Eve, are described as perambulating at their marriage ceremony.

Another variety of this type is the Otori shrine, which has two pillars instead of one, with connecting partitions to the side walls, thus forming one room in front of the other, the inner one being used as the sanctuary. The worshippers are here in front of the divine emblem instead of at the side of it as in the Izumo shrine. And when the outer chamber is made about half as large again as the inner we have the style of the Sumiyoshi shrine. And there is a type of farm-house corresponding to the Otori style, that known as Kuni-naka-sumai, where the main portion of the building has these two pillars. An example of a house that is apparently a survival of the Izumo plan is that in Amatsu village of Tansei district of the province of Echizen. It is 21 by 36 feet and is divided into two parts, the inner one with a wooden floor covered with matting and the outer with a floor of hard earth. This outer space is called Oi or O Yue, dialetic for O Ie, the House Place. The left side is called the Upper House (O Yue no kami) and the right the Lower House (O Yue no shimo). In the centre is the hearth and in the middle of the floored part is the Daikyoku Bashira or Centre Pillar. The fact that the lower part is called the House Place suggests that it was the original building with the hearth in its centre, and that the inner part was added later. This inner part consists of two rooms, one of ten mats with an alcove and Buddhist shrine, which is the main reception room, and another six-mat chamber beside it called Nando. This Nando is the original of the Chōdai or canopied dais found in the residence of Imperial Personages and Court nobles, and is still so called in the country. Nando means the place where things are put, i.e. clothes, therefore dressing-room and so bedroom. Another name for it is Kakima, which is evidently a corruption of Kage-no-ma

---

[3] It is called the "umbrella shape."

(dark room). Behind this there is a three-mat room in which the Buddhist priest is accommodated when he pays a visit, otherwise used as a storeroom. The space of earth by the entrance is where guests are received, and the doorless and usually wall-less *pissoir* outside it is common in farm-houses, and is there for purely practical purposes, for fertilizer is valuable.

Examples of the Otori style may be seen in many ancient dwellings to be found in the Iga district, Shiga Prefecture, of which Plate 5 Fig. 1 is one of the simplest. Here the inner part is one foot higher than the outer and the two rooms in it have a ceiling. The outer part is used to receive ordinary guests, and the inner especially favoured ones. The sitting-room (*d*) has its floor covered with bran about two inches deep, with straw matting laid over it. This room is called Nyuji, the meaning of which is unknown. It is also called Omote (exterior). The inner rooms (*e*) and (*f*) are called Oku (interior) and have a wood floor. Modern hygiene has brought about the abolition of the bran covering and matting in favour of a board floor, but this is still kept half a foot or so lower than that of the inner room, so that, counting the *tokonoma,* the house has three levels like the Jodan, Chudan and Gedan in the mansion of a noble. These houses of Iga have mud walls and most of them still have only small lattice windows with neither *shōji* nor *amado,* while inside they have wooden sliding doors instead of *fusuma.* It was not till the Ashikaga age that these were introduced in the capital and later still in the provinces. Till then the Japanese house had none of the characteristics we now associate with it and did not differ much from the European cottage. These people do not reckon the size of the rooms by the number of *tatami* or mats (for they have none, since they belong to the pre-tatami period), but by the number of widths of matting from the edge of the raised floor to the threshold beam. Four of these would be about eight *tatami,* which is the usual size of these rooms.[4]

The influence of these early dwellings is apparent also in the arrangement of the first Buddhist temples, since these were simply houses in which Buddhas were installed. For instance, it is recorded in the *Nihon Shoki* that a certain Wakaomi-no-Azumabito of Shinano

[4] The *Chou Li* says that the Ming Tang was nine mats east to west and seven north to south. It is possible that the 9 feet length of these may be about the same as that of the Japanese *tatami*.

went to the capital in the days of the Emperor Kōgyoku and brought back an image of Buddha which he installed in his house, and this is the beginning of the famous temple of Zenkōji. It is not so remarkable that, situated as it is in a remote district, this temple should have preserved definite traces of the plan of an ancient residence, as pointed out by Dr Kida in his research into the relations between temples, shrines and residences in Japan. The Main Hall (Hondo) of the Zenkōji is a building 58 yards long from north to south, but only 30 yards wide from east to west. It has, of course, been considerably lengthened since it was first founded, and does not now resemble the original building; but Dr Kida considers that the north end in which the image of Amida Buddha stands probably represents the early temple which was entered from the eastern end and was therefore a building just like that of the Izumo shrine. Afterwards, when the front entrance developed, this temple was altered to conform to the fashion. This inner part of the sanctuary measures just 18 feet square.

The type of house entered in front like the Ise shrine is the commonest and is found everywhere. The example here given is, however, a very old type at Hase in the neighbourhood of Kyoto. The interior plan is still the same, but there is an addition at the side of an earth-floored kitchen space in which is the stove and a wooden bench (*shōgi*) at which meals are taken. This house has no verandas (*engawa*) except before the reception room. The walls are all of plaster, with few windows, and there is no ceiling. The Nando has plastered walls with no window and is quite dark. It was formerly actually used to sleep in, but is now only used as a storeroom. It is the custom in Kyoto, even in the large merchants' houses, for the master and his servants to take their meals on this wooden bench in the earth-floored kitchen court, a survival from the days before the floors were boarded and matted. The Shishinden (ceremonial hall) of the palace was formerly without a ceiling, which was in those days lacking everywhere. Most farm-houses and many dwellings in the towns also have still no ceiling in the kitchen and often in other rooms as well. And Japanese have always liked the effect of this open roof, properly dressed (*kesho-yaneura*), and affect it much in verandas, tea-rooms and corridors.

These examples show that the shrine was simply the ancient Japanese residence and it will be noted, too, that farm-houses, like shrines, are very often surrounded by a grove. The word *mori* (grove) is explained by Miyasaki in his *Dictionary of Foreign Words* as equivalent to the Korean *ma-lin* meaning "forbidding" or "protecting." And in the *Manyoshu* the expression *kinden* (forbidden fields) is read in Japanese as *morita*, while the same text has *mori* for *jinja* (shrine). So *mori* is likely to mean the protecting hedge round a dwelling or shrine, and it is significant that the Deity Susa-no-O, who is an Izumo Deity, goes to Korea and lives in a place called Soshi-mori, the *mori* of which probably means "abode." And in the village of Tsutsu in Tsushima there is still to be seen a grove of oak-trees with an altar in the middle, which is exactly the same as the Shiki-no-Himorogi mentioned in the annals of the Emperor Sujin as erected to worship the Sun Goddess. This Himorogi is an enclosure of trees with an altar in the centre in which the presence of the Deity is held to be manifest. It is still used where there is no shrine and it seems likely that it was the earliest place of worship before a residence was set aside for the Deity. The word *himorogi* is explained as equivalent to *mi-muro-gi* (trees of the divine abode) and *shiki* as the same as *suki*, also "abode." The grove in Tsushima is called Shigi by the villagers, which is quite likely the same word. This Himorogi is not peculiar to Japan either, for in the *Chou Li* in the days of Confucius a description of the same thing is found. It is just that worship "under the blue vault of heaven"[5] that many still prefer. And the Japanese Shinto shrine has never been a congregational building. It is the abode of the Deity which the worshippers approach but do not enter. Its later developments were entirely the result of the influence of the Buddhist connexion. Its resemblance to a Greek temple will no doubt already have occurred to most—except that it never housed an image but only a symbol. One may perhaps conjecture that the Izumo type of shrine, the square umbrella style, was introduced through Korean influence, while the Ise type represents a Polynesian variety that came in with the invaders from the south.

In the latter connexion mention may be made of the unique buildings at Iwase at Shirakawa, in the province of Hida on the borders of Shinano and Echizen, one of the most remote parts of the country deep in the mountain ranges where few outsiders have penetrated.

---

[5] Images and pictures of Shinto Deities are sometimes found, especially of the Gods of Good Luck and Tenjin, the God of Letters, but they are not put in shrines.

These big residences contain a very large family including relations, more than thirty people in all, and look like a survival of the Polynesian long-house (in Japanese *nagaya* [long-house], is the word for barrack or tenement), in which a whole village community lives. And the roofs are extremely steep, some 60 degrees or more, just like that of the Izumo shrine and the older buildings before the less acute Chinese type of roof was introduced and popularized in the Nara period. Few of the more modern Japanese roofs have a slope of more than 45 degrees owing to this influence, and as the result of wood and tile coverings instead of the earlier thatch which shrines nearly always retain, though now it is usually thick shingle. The Emperor Yūryaku (A.D. 457-480), in whose days intercourse with the neighbouring lands was very flourishing, is described as ordering a "storied pavilion" to be built, though no details are given of it. But in the days of the Emperor Suinin something of the kind was apparently not unknown because there is in the *Kōjiki* a passage in which his younger sister O-Naka-hime declares she cannot climb into the Ama-no-hokora because she is a weak woman and he replies that a ladder can be made. It must have been the sort of building depicted on the mirror dug up at Kariai village in the Katsuragi district of Yamato province. (Plate 1 Fig 2.) Polynesian houses, high like these early shrines, are often entered by a notched log which does not look very easy to climb. Yūryaku Tenno was contemporary with the Six Dynasties of China and in one of the works of this period, called *Liang Chou Lai Tien,* it is stated that they had communication with Pacific lands from a distance of five thousand *li* to twenty or thirty thousand.

Hokora is the Japanese word still used for a small shrine. It seems to contain the word *kura,* found in Taka-mi-kura (the Imperial Throne), which is like a small raised enclosure with a canopy. It may therefore mean "a raised place" and is compared by Fujita with the word *uran,* which is said to be used of a pavilion by some unknown southern country in the *Liang Dynasty Records of the Southern Countries.*

CHAPTER III

THE INTRODUCTION OF BUDDHISM
ASUKA PERIOD (540-640)

IT was the introduction of Buddhism that brought architecture to Japan with the crafts of painting and sculpture, metal-work and ceramics. Chinese writing may well have been known already, but not very much and to few people. Buddhism was first brought to Japan in 522 by one Shiba Tachito, a Chinese from Southern Liang, where it was very fashionable. He set up a chapel with an image and the great Minister Soga-no-Iname also gave his house to be used for the same purpose. Then in the sixth year of the Emperor Bidatsu (578) there arrived monks and Buddha-makers and temple artisans from Kudara, the western part of Korea. So the Minister Soga-no-Umako, son of Iname, was able to build a pagoda of some sort on the hill of Ono in Yamato, the first of many of its kind—but nothing remains of it but a few stones and tiles, for it was burnt by the opposition.

However, when Buddhists once more gained a footing, having overcome the objections of the conservative military party which was as anti-foreign and pro-Shinto as it usually is, a number of leading scholars came from the continent in the days of the Empress Suiko (593-628) equipped with all the knowledge of science and the arts as then developed; and before a century had passed since its first appearance Buddhism could count forty-six temples, eight hundred and sixty monks and five hundred and sixty-nine nuns. But of this period little has been left but names, for the buildings themselves are of later date and only the Kondo (main hall), the pagoda, the middle gate and the cloisters of the great monastery of Hōryuji, and the pagoda of the Hokkiji have survived. Indeed it is a wonder that so much is still to be seen, since they are all wooden buildings and in Japan fires and wars and earthquakes are endemic.

What is rather remarkable is that the Hōryuji is the only building that remains anywhere to show what the style of the wooden structures of the North and South dynasties in China, transmitted through Korea, was like. Similarly the Yume-dono of the same monastery is the only surviving ancient Korean building, for none are left in that country itself. Japan is indeed a museum of ancient Far Eastern civilizations.

The Hōryuji represents what is called the Kudara style "Temple of Seven Halls" (Kudara-shiki Shichido Garan). It was a combination of college and infirmary and temple. In front it had a large court or cloister and it faced the south. All these early temples are approached by a Nandaimon (Southern Great Gate). The great hall and the pagoda stand in the cloister and behind them is the library and the bell-tower. Behind this is the lecture hall (Kōdō) and on the north, east and west are the residences of the monks.

There are two plans of this style, the one that has the main hall and pagoda built on a straight line running through the middle gate and lecture hall like the ancient Korean temples and the Shitennoji at Osaka in Japan, and the Hōryuji type that has them set on each side of this line. It is possible that these buildings may have been rebuilt after a fire as some allege; but even so there is no reason to doubt that they are anything but genuine specimens of Asuka work, for they are quite different from the productions of the Nara age.[1] Moreover, their decorations and the Buddhist statuary do not seem to have been damaged. A set of eaves has been added at a later date to the lower part of the Kondo for protection against the weather and the fenestration somewhat altered. Professor Amanuma's drawing represents it as it was in its original state. The dragon-carved struts in the upper part and the ornaments in the gable ends were added in the Edo period and look like it.[2] The Kondo stands on a stone base and its round pillars have entasis. They have no bases but stand on natural stones resembling the Greek Doric order. Their greatest diameter is about a third from the bottom, and they diminish in circumference only slightly toward the base, whereas they do so much more toward the top, their

---

[1] Dr Sekino has, moreover, discovered that the Kondo is built with the Korean foot measure which was prohibited after 645.

[2] It may be interesting to compare the awful marble Gilbert Scott screen and pulpit in Durham Cathedral, which an indulgent dean and chapter allow to remain an eyesore in the noble Norman nave.

proportions being therefore not unlike those of the Corinthian column. On the top of the pillars are round plates (*sarato*), and on these again the bracket capitals. The pillars have no connexion with the upper story, the eaves have no ceiling and the rafters no particular method of arrangement. The elbow brackets are of the simplest form, but at the corners they are prolonged in a cloud shape and are so called "cloud brackets" (*kumo hijiki*). The simpler form is called "ship bracket" (*funa hijiki*). Beneath the bressummer beam of the upper story is a species of strut that is the earliest form of the characteristic "frog-crotch (*kaeru-mata*). These details are almost exactly identical with those of the rock carvings of the Tat'ung caves in Shansi province in China, famous as survivals of the North Wei style of architecture which derived from the Gupta era in India (fifth century).[3]

The balustrade of the upper part has a swastika design which is also unique. It seems likely that the ridge had originally "kite-tail" terminals (*shibi*) like those of the Tamamushi shrine which is preserved in the Kondo. It is a model of a building of this type, 7 feet high, said to have been the private shrine of the Empress Suiko, and to have been formerly in the Tachibana temple. It has square pillars and round rafters, but in this only it differs from the Kondo. Its name comes from the covering of the wings of beetles (*tamamushi*) that was once under the metal openwork overlay. The paintings on it are of Buddhist scenes done in Chinese style with some kind of oil. Altogether it is a very remarkable work of art.

The Hōryuji pagoda is the earliest in Japan. The Japanese word *tō* (pagoda) is short for *sotoba,* from the Sanskrit *stupa*—just as the word *garan*, used in early days for Buddhist temples, is short for *sōga-rama* (*sangharama*). The purpose of this tower is either to indicate a sacred site or to contain a Buddhist relic. In Japan it was for the latter purpose and not simply for ornament. The Indian stupa is the mound-shaped tomb of a great person surmounted by a royal throne with an umbrella on top of it, as seen in Sanchi and the Ajanta cave chapels. In China and Japan the relic was originally in the receptacle on the pinnacle of the spire, so this part was considered the most important and emphasized accordingly, while the central member developed into

---

[3] Also in the Korean tomb of the sixth century illustrated in Eckardt's *Korean Art*, p. xxxiii, which has also lotus capital pillars, and a roof with diagonal slabs like the base of an Indian dome.

the three, five or seven stories that distinguish the Far Eastern variety. In China they are made of brick and stone; and smaller ones are sometimes found in Japan of the latter material, but never full-sized ones. The stupa base has disappeared altogether in this ordinary type but appears again in the Daito and Hōto type introduced in the ninth century. This is of the same variety as the Tibetan *chorten,* with the difference that wooden construction naturally produces. In Japan the lowest story of a pagoda is used as a chapel and decorated in gilt and colours. This one is a five-storied structure with just the same architectural features as the Kondo and, like it, erected on a stone stylobate.

The colonnade that surrounds the cloister is very simply and harmoniously constructed with dressed rafters, exhibiting a very early form of *kōryo* or curved tie-beam connecting the tops of the pillars, on the heads of which are the three-branch brackets characteristic of this style. The lines of these brackets have the same gentle curve as the elbow, unlike those of later date. In the centre of this tie-beam is the same frog-crotch as is found in the balustrade. The pagoda of the Hokkiji is also a fine specimen and the largest of the three-storied variety. Its wide eaves have a comparatively gentle curve and its proportions are most graceful, more so in fact than any of similar type. Its details are the same as those of the Hōryuji.[4]

As to the Shi-Tennoji at Osaka, it has none of its original buildings left, though it was the first temple to be built, and was begun as the result of a vow by Prince Shōtoku that he would build a temple to the Four Deva Kings (Shi-Tenno) if he won the fight against Moriya, chief of the Mononobe or military caste. The present buildings are of the Momoyama and Edo periods, not earlier than the sixteenth century. But in their plan they have preserved the original form, and the Nandaimon (Great South Gate), the middle gate (Chūmon) the pagoda, the Kondo and the Kōdō are all in a straight line in that order across the quadrangle. Shōtoku Taishi built seven temples beside the Shi-Tennoji and the Hōryuji. The Chuguji, the Tachibana-dera, the Hachioka-dera, the Ikejiri-dera, the Katsuragi-dera, for instance, and besides these there are the Kumagori, Yamada and Kume temples of

[4] The curve in the roof of Chinese buildings is best explained as partly functional, to ward off sun and rain, and partly influenced by the downward brush-stroke of Chinese calligraphy.

this period, most of them long ago destroyed or rebuilt. On the tiles of the Hōryuji and in some other parts of it are designs of honeysuckle and vine scrolls (*karakusa*) of the same kind as those in the Parthenon and on Greek vases. The vine scroll pattern is not found in Korea and so has evidently come from Gandhara work by way of China. These temples were painted red with the ends of the beams yellow and the balustrades of the balconies green. The interiors were plastered and decorated in colours also—green, red, purple, black and brown. There is little carved work in the Hōryuji. The ends of the rafters where they project are plain and have no elephant-headed ornaments or patterns like the later structures, but there are in some places metal mounts of openwork on these beams. The ends of the balustrade rails, again, are quite straight and have not the upward curve usually seen later.

The only architectural survivals of the Asuka era are therefore the temples, and nothing remains to show what the capital was like but tradition and a few foundation stones. According to this evidence the capital of Asuka lay across the plain south of Nara between Mount Unebi (near which is the mausoleum of Jimmu Tenno) and Ama-no-Kaguyama famous in the *Manyōshu*. It is conjectured that the city was laid out on the same plan as that of Nara, but with twelve avenues, the great central Shujaku Avenue leading to the Fujiwara palace of the Empress Jito and the Emperor Mommu, with the Daikyoku Den or Great Hall of Audience. Round about it are the mausolea of many Emperors. Judging from the architecture of the temples, the palace buildings might well have been quite imposing, though some also may have been of the simple style of the shrines, for there is mention of a Kuroki-no-miya (natural wood palace) by Tenchi Tenno (668), though this may have been a detached one. But the Asuka palace of the Empress Kōgyoku (642) was roofed with boards, and that of the Empress Saimei (655) was the first to be covered with tiles.

CHAPTER IV

HAKUHŌ PERIOD (640-720)

By this time the South and North period in China had given place to the Sui dynasty, a short one chiefly noted for the luxurious Emperor who built many temples and excavated the Grand Canal. Then this passed to make way for the famous dynasty of T'ang under the Emperor Tai Tsung, when the Middle Kingdom reached the zenith of her greatness and made her influence felt from the Yellow Sea to the confines of Persia.

Japan, as might be expected of her, at once threw herself wholeheartedly into importing and adapting this brilliant civilization to her own needs, and the Hakuhō[1] period was the result. The name Taika or Great Reform was given to this process of sinicization which was much the same as the Meiji Restoration of 1868, except that the T'ang culture was no doubt more compatible with conditions in Japan than was European, and its architecture more easily adapted than, for example, that of the continental Renaissance. It suited the climate and could be carried out in wood. Little remains now of the T'ang era in China except what is excavated or written, so that again we can see more of its works in Japan than in the country of its origin. There are no traces of Sui style in Japan, but at once in the Hakuhō period we find the T'ang variety of the Shichido Garan or Temple of Seven Halls.

This has two pagodas facing each other, often inside the quadrangle, at a little distance from the centre line of the buildings through the south gate, which is as before. In the earlier day they are not as regular as in the later Tempyo period: for example, the Kōfukuji at Nara has its eastern pagoda of four stories and its western of three. At Yakushiji both are similarly placed inside the cloister as in the Kudara style, so that it may be said that this period has the character

---

[1] Hakuhō means white phoenix.

of a transition from Asuka to Tempyo. The buildings stand on a stone stylobate with square bases to the pillars which have a slight entasis. Square pillars are used in the upper story and the bracketing is three-branched.

The buildings of the Kōfukuji, built by Fujiwara Fuhito in 712 as a chapel for his family, are all modern, for it has been burnt many times. But a remarkable relic of this time is the three-storied pagoda at Yakushiji. Originally there were two, but only the eastern pagoda has survived, and of the western only the foundation stones remain. The detail of the bracketing is reminiscent of the Asuka style, but the eaves are ceiled and the lowest chamber has a coved ceiling, both innovations. It is unique among Japanese pagodas for having double eaves to each story, the same construction as the roof of the Hōryuji Kondo, and a throw-back to the Asuka style. Japanese critics consider it very elegant and rhythmic in its proportions and one writer lauds it as "frozen music." This peculiarity gives it the appearance of having six stories, an even number, whereas all others except the Tahōtō type have an odd number of stories. It is 120 feet high, the *sōrin* or spire comprising 20 feet of this and having on its top an elaborate iron "spray" like the decoration of a weathercock; but with a design of three Buddhist angels with flowing robes, one playing a flute, the second scattering perfume, and the third lotus flowers. A very interesting relic is the model pagoda of the Kairyuōji, now in the Nara museum, a miniature edition of the actual edifice which has fortunately escaped destruction. It must be one of the oldest wooden architectural models in existence. The dearth of relics of this age is mostly due to the removal of the capital to Nara, whither some of the buildings were transferred, but most were allowed to fall into ruin.

CHAPTER V

TEMPYO PERIOD (720-780)

THE Emperor Mommu had decided to move the capital again and in the reign of his successor, the Empress Gemmyo, it was changed to the site of Nara on the north side of the plain under the foot of Mount Mikasa, and here it remained until 794, during the reigns of seven Sovereigns. This is the golden age of Buddhist architecture and sculpture for more of the resources of the country were spent on these things than ever afterwards. This was because of the immense enthusiasm of the Sovereign and the Court for the Indian philosophy. Nara was certainly a city of monks and temples, and a contemporary account says that, looking down on it from Wakagusa hill more than fifty pagodas could be counted rearing their graceful spires aloft, conspicuous among them the two great seven-storied ones of the Tōdaiji, 320 feet high, and another at the Gankōji of 240 feet. Nara had seven great temples: the Tōdaiji, the Saidaiji, the Daianji, the Kōfukuji, the Gankōji, the Yakushiji, and the Toshōdaiji. But of all their extensive buildings but little now remains. Even the Great Buddha of the Tōdaiji has been burnt three times and his head melted off, so that only his body is of this period.

By this time the T'ang type of temple had been perfected and the twin eastern and western pagodas stood outside the cloister equidistant on east and west. The Kondo stood in the centre of the quadrangle of the first court entered by the middle gate through the outer south gate as before. Through a second gate lay the inner court in which were the belfry and the library, equidistant from the axis of the court. Behind these again was the Kōdō. The details of the construction are now fully developed, but entirely functional and quite without fussiness. The pillars are round with a slight bulge and the bracket capitals of the three-branch type. The soffits of the rafters and the interior ceilings are coved and ribbed (*shirin*). The curved ties have simple uncarved frog-crotches and straight struts alternating with them. The spacing of the pillars and the fenestration give these buildings a very restful and dignified air, as can be well seen from the façades of the Kondo and Kōdō of the Toshōdaiji. The latter building is said to have been one of the halls of the Imperial Palace which was presented to this temple. The Great Buddha Hall or Kondo of the Tōdaiji is the largest wooden building in the world, but it does not belong to this period, since it was reconstructed in the Tenjiku style of the Kamakura era. Only part of the Hokkedo (a wing was added to it in the Kamakura style), the library of the Kangakuin, and the Tengai gate of this temple are of the Nara age. The finest specimens of the period are the Toshōdaiji, the Yume-dono and library and refectory of the Hōryuji, the eastern pagoda of the Tomado and the octagonal hall (Hakkakudo) of the Eisanji. The Hokkedo is really older than the Tōdaiji itself, for it was built by Archbishop Ryōben in the fifth year of Tempyo (733) and has survived all the rest.

The Toshōdaiji was the work of Kanshin, a Chinese monk, on the site of the residence of Prince Nitabe which the Emperor Shōmu gave him. Its Kondo is perhaps the finest specimen of the architecture of the Nara age. As in all the other temples, the roof is of the single *azumaya* or hipped type with kite-tail finials. In the front the pillars are arranged to form a colonnade. It was painted red outside with green window bars and the cove of the ceiling was decorated with vine scroll patterns and Buddhist figures, while the pillars are also ornamented with designs of flowers and flying Bodhisats.

The Kōdo was originally, it is said, the Chōshuden of the palace, presented by the Empress Kōken of great piety. Among other things it had originally no ceiling, only the tie-beam and frog-crotch construction under the dressed rafters; but when rebuilt as the lecture hall of the temple a coffered ceiling was added. The doors and lattice windows are of the Kamakura age and the bracketing and struts have also been altered somewhat. The 240-foot pagoda of the Gankōji and the main hall were standing until the eighteen twenties when they were burnt, but a woodcut that remains, reproduced by Professor Amanuma, shows very fine and stately proportions.

Nara also contains one quite unique structure, the Shōsōin or log-built storehouse in which have reposed, ever since the death of the Emperor Shōmu, all the furniture and utensils that he had used and which were presented to the Tōdaiji by the Empress Kōmyo for the perfection of his enlightenment. There were many other storehouses of the same construction in other temples too, but few have survived and it is remarkably providential that this one, the most valuable of all, should have been preserved, though it has had some narrow escapes.[1] There is no other collection in the world like it, for these are not excavated objects, but have always been above ground where they now are and their condition is excellent. They have been catalogued and annotated and there are some three thousand articles in all,[2] comprising furniture, dress, weapons, food utensils, games, musical instruments and writings, pictures and Buddhist statuettes. Besides objects of Japanese workmanship they include Korean, Chinese and even Indian and Persian specimens presented to the Chinese Emperor, and thence sent to Japan. Belonging to the Imperial Household, they could not be viewed even by the Shogun without the Imperial Permission. This construction of logs is called Azekura[3] and is made of three-cornered lengths interlocked. It stands on big round pillars 9 feet high on large stone bases. The space beneath it gives good ventilation and the method of construction is such that in summer the heat contracts the timbers and lets in the breeze through the interstices, while in winter the damp expands them and keeps the interior dry. And as the projecting edges of these beams are triangular the birds are quite unable to build nests in them. All these qualities, say the Japanese commentators, make this Azekura style ideal for storehouses. The timber is *hinoki* and it is worn down an inch and a half outside by the weathering of some twelve hundred and fifty years.

Within the precincts of the Hōryuji are preserved two other fine relics of the Tempyo age. These are the Yume-dono and the Dempōdō of the Tōin temple built in 739 on the site of the Ikaruga palace of Prince Shōtoku. The Yume-dono (Hall of Dreams) is the Kondo of the temple and the Dempōdō is the Kōdō. The former is a graceful octagonal building standing on a stone stylobate of two tiers with a railed veranda round it. The interior has a stone floor and a base

---

[1] In 1256 there was a fire, which the monks fought ferociously and in the end successfully. This escape was attributed to the favour of the Sea Deity.

[2] A fine selection of them has been reproduced in colour in the three volumes published by the Shimbi Shōin Company.

[3] Probably from *azanau* to interlace the fingers, i.e. in the Shingon ritual.

made of a kind of concrete. On the top of the roof, which is of the pyramidal type, there is an uncommon finial consisting of a jar-shaped vessel on a lotus throne having a canopy with wind-bells over it, and on that again a jewel top. It is the *kalasha* or nectar pot (called also by the Japanese *rōban* or dew pot, the first syllable being for *kanrō* or nectar) which is a feature of the spires of Hindu temples.[4] There is another on the top of the pagoda of the Murōji, but this is the earliest and they are rare. The Dempōdō is interesting also for having been, according to tradition, the residence of the Lady Tachibana, mother of the Empress Kōmyo. It is a single-roofed gabled building with a veranda in front and a wooden floor, neither of which things are found in the temple halls of this age. Thus it is a rare specimen of the residence of a noble in the early eighth century. Of a similar type is the Kondo of the Shin-Yakushiji, burnt after a few years, but rebuilt soon afterwards. The pagoda and the rest of it are of the Kamakura age. It is peculiar in having a round Buddha altar stuccoed in white standing on the usual stone floor.

On the whole, the interior decoration of this period is far more developed than that of the previous ones. The pillars and ceilings are very finely painted and the outside is red as before. There is little if any carving in the temples and only some openwork metal mounts. All this colour is, of course, quite continental, and Japanese taste had not yet eliminated it.

THE CAPITAL OF HEIJO

Owing to the greater solidity of the architecture as well as the increasing complication of life that had resulted from the introduction of continental civilization and the improvement of communications, it seems to have been felt that the shifting of the capital with the reign was far from convenient. So when, in 708, the capital was moved to Nara, a far more permanent kind of building was adopted both for the palace and for the better class of residence. By 724 the palace and the

---

[4] According to Havell's *Indian Architecture* (p. 16): "The nectar pot or *kalasha* holds the nectar of immortality, churned by the gods and demons from the cosmic ocean. . . .

"The combination of lotus flower, bell-shaped seed capsule and water pot forms the basis of the design of most Hindoo temple pillars, the prototypes of which were doubtless the carved wooden posts marking the sacrificial area in the ancient Vedic rites."

great temples had been rebuilt there. Other structures must have been of a more temporary nature, for an edict was issued by the Dajokan or Cabinet suggesting that officials of the fifth rank and upwards and other substantial families should roof their houses with tiles, plaster them white, and paint them red.

This capital has of course quite disappeared but, principally through the investigations of Professors Kida and Sekino, most of its details have been made fairly clear except in some cases—as for instance the width of the streets. It was laid out on the model of the T'ang capital of Chang An, but its greatest length was from north to south instead of from east to west as in that city, while the use of numbers for its streets instead of names was a Japanese innovation. It was laid out in the Handen or chequer-board fashion, i.e. divided into *jō* or avenues of four *chō* in width, east to west and north to south. These *jō* were again divided into *bō* of four *chō* square, sixteen *chō* thus going to a *bō*. These were again divided into sixteen *tsubo*. The city was nine *jō* from north to south and eight *bō* from east to west. Right down the middle from the south gate to the gate of the government quarter in the north ran the wide central highway called the Shujaku, dividing the city into the left and right capitals (Sakyo and Ukyo). Then every four *chō*, parallel with the Shujaku went another wide street (*ōji*) while narrow streets (*koji*) divided the *chō*. The wide street at the end of the fourth *bō* was called *Kyōgoku* or City Limit. From the second avenue of the left capital to the fifth was an extension of three *bō* called the outer capital (Gekyo) within which the great temples of the Kōfukuji, and Gankōji were situated. The Imperial Enclosure occupied four *chō* at the north end. On the south side of it was the Shujaku gate, and twelve other gates gave entrance to it on the four sides. Within was the palace with the Chōdōin and Daikyoku Den or Halls of Ceremony and Audience, where the great festivals were held and entertainments were given. The foundations of many of these buildings have been excavated recently and their sites determined, but with the exceptions above mentioned nothing is left of them. Probably they were not very different from those of Heian. The palace itself was built on an elevation with a view of the Yamato mountains.

CHAPTER VI

HEIAN PERIOD (780-1190)

THE Heian period comprises the four centuries that elapsed from the removal of the capital from Nara to the fall of the Heike house, perhaps more accurately 805-1192. The influence of the T'ang civilization still continued, but a very considerable modification was caused by the introduction of Tendai and Shingon Buddhism—the Esoteric System (Mikkyo), as it is called—by the two great ecclesiastics Dengyo and Kōbō. Moreover the T'angs were decidedly on the decline and so Japan ceased to regard them with the same respect as formerly. The Shingon strain brought in a more austere type of building, and soon after this the intercourse with the T'angs ceased altogether and the golden age of the Fujiwara Regents inaugurated a more luxurious habit of building and developed incidentally a pure Japanese style by eliminating all that was not in accordance with the national taste.

This period is conveniently divided into the first century from the foundation of the Heian capital to the accession of the Emperor Uda in 897, called the Kōnin era, and the later three centuries from that time to 1192, usually known as the Fujiwara period—four centuries of peace and prosperity, and for the Court and officials considerable luxury, in which the arts and crafts could be cultivated. The first period is a transition from Tempyo to Fujiwara, rather like the early Nara age that led up to Tempyo.

Tendai Buddhism was founded by Dengyo Daishi who went to China and studied on Mount Tientai, whence the name, and Shingon or Tantric Buddhism by Kōbō Daishi who also went there.[1] and these sects required a different kind of temple from those so far prevailing.

---

[1] Wars that supervened in China prevented any more students being sent. Wu Sung, a contemporary of the Emperor Uda, destroyed Buddhist temples everywhere, which explains why there are none of this period in China. He destroyed what there was of Nestorian Christianity too.

Dengyo built Hieizan on the mountain of that name to the north-west of the capital, to protect it from the demons who are reputed to attack from that quarter, though later on the monks assumed their function; but Kōbō founded his establishment on Mount Koya in the province of Kii, far from all inhabited parts. A flat site in a capital was not a suitable place to meditate on profound philosophies; and since these remote mountain peaks were chosen for monasteries it was not possible to keep to the older conventional regular form at all. The monasteries had to be arranged to fit their environment, and the halls placed often on different levels, where any small flat place for them could be found: "sites in the hills no bigger than a cat's forehead," is the Japanese description. There were very few places like Mount Koya, where there is quite an extensive plateau on the hill. Most were like Hieizan, where the buildings were scattered irregularly up and down, and in some cases had to be built out from the rocks and supported on trestles from below.

This age saw the introduction of a new kind of pagoda. This was the Daito which had a square lower story with the usual pyramidal roof; but superimposed on this, as though emerging from it, is a round dome called a "turtle belly," crowned by a round balustrade over which again is a roof with a spire supported on pillars. There are also two other varieties of stupa, the Sōrinto and the Yūgito, the former a Tendai speciality and the latter peculiar to Shingon. The Sōrinto is a simple stupa pillar or *stambha*[2] and the Yūgito, named after Yūgi Bosatsu because a picture of it is on a portrait of him, is a stupa reliquary with a top like that of the Daito, but with a round base with doors under the turtle's belly, the whole standing on a turtle's back. On the roof are five spires, one on each angle of it and one in the middle. It is described as a pagoda of five peaks and eight pillars, symbolical perhaps of the Noble Eightfold Path and the Five Prohibitions. Professor Amanuma, who, from an old picture, has constructed one lately at the Ryūkoin, the temple on Mount Koya where Kōbō Daishi lived, points out that the Amravati Dagoba has four pillars a side with a rail between in just this style.

The great temples of this early Kōnin era were the Enryakuji on Mount Hiei, the Kongobuji on Mount Kōya, and the Kyōō Gōkokuji

---

[2] Like the Asoka and other pillars in India.

now called Tōji, Ninnaji, Murōji and Kiyomizu-dera in Kyoto; but all that remains of the period is the Kondo and five-storied pagoda of the Murōji. There was a decided development of shrine architecture at this time under the influence of Buddhism. The types that are new are the Kasuga style, the Nagare or Yuiitsu style, the Hiyoshi and the Hachiman styles.

The Kasuga shrine is a gabled building with a lean-to porch supported on pillars and covering the front steps, which are in the centre of the gable. The roof, like that of most shrines, now takes on the curve associated with Buddhist temples. The Shimmei style is merely a modified form of the Ise type, with one side of the roof brought right forward over the front steps, and more ornamental balustrades. Both this and the former one are painted red, thus departing from the simplicity of the plain grey wood of Ise and Izumo. The Kamo shrine, too, is of this type. The actual buildings of these shrines are not old, but like Ise and Izumo shrines they have always been rebuilt in the same form. In these later types the characteristic cross-beams (*chigi* and *katsuōgi*) are omitted and the roof approximates to that of a temple; or if they are present they are not functional at all but merely applied ornaments. The Hachiman style has a gabled shrine 18 feet deep, with a second one 6 feet deep built in front of it and connected with it by an ante-chamber. The Hiyoshi type is an 18-foot-deep shrine with the roof brought down over the steps in front and eaves projecting on both sides, looking like an *irimoya* roof at the ends and a gabled one in front. It has a veranda round it.

THE HEIAN CAPITAL

The Emperor Kammu moved the capital from Nara to Nagaoka in Yamashiro in 784; and there it remained for ten years, when it was moved once more to the village of Uda, also in Yamashiro province, where the new palace and city were built and finished by 804. This was called the Capital of Heian (Heian no Miyako), usually called Miyako or "the Capital" since it continued to be so till 1870 when the military capital of Edo became the Imperial Residence under the name of Tōkyo or Eastern Capital. The old capital was then called Kyoto, or very often Saikyo or Western Capital by the people of western Japan, just as Nara was usually known in medieval times as Nankyo or Southern Capital.

The reason for the change is said to have been the Emperor's desire to escape from the oppressive atmosphere of the monasteries of Nara. The new site was certainly a good one, a flat plain by the river Kamo which communicated with the river Yodo and the sea, surrounded by hills on the east, west and north and comparatively close to Lake Biwa to the east. The other sites had not been so well supplied with waterways. The new city was laid out on the same plan as that of Nara, with the Shujaku highway down the centre dividing it into left and right capitals. It was about three and a half miles long north to south and three miles east to west. It had the same nine avenues. The Great Highway was 250 feet wide and the other avenues were 80 feet wide, except the first and ninth (Ichijo and Kujo) which were 120, Nijo, which was 170, and four others between the first and ninth, which were 100 feet wide. Similarly the transverse streets running parallel with the Shujaku, those at the extremities, the east and west Kyōgoku, and two others were 120 and the rest 80 feet wide. The smaller lanes were 40 feet wide. The city unit was a block of 400 feet square called a *chō,* which was normally divided into thirty-two residential areas of 50 by 100 feet. Four of these blocks went to a *hō* or square and again four *hō* made a *bō* or division. The *bō* was the square space between two *jō* or avenues, and there were four of them, as in Nara, between the Great Highway and the Kyōgoku or city boundary on the east and west. On the south at the end of the central highway was the Rasho-mon or Great Gate of the city, 54 feet wide with seven portals; while at the north end, as before, was the Shujaku gate of the palace enclosure.

The whole city was surrounded by an embankment and ditch and was intersected from south to north by the east and west Horikawa, the east and west Omiyagawa, the Sakigawa, and the west Dōingawa streams, which were canalized and made to flow so that they added considerably to the amenities of the city. On each side of the Rasho-mon stood the East and West Temples, Tōji and Saiji, and in front of the palace enclosure was the Imperial Pleasure Park (Shinen) and the University (Daigaku). The palace enclosure extended from Ichijo to Nijo, 1533 yards from north to south and 1266 from east to west. Within were the Dairi or Imperial Residence and all the government departments as before. There were fourteen gates, four on the east and west and three on the south and north sides.

Two large buildings inside the palace were the Chōdōin, used for the accession ceremony and other important Court functions, and the Burakuin where the Imperial Entertainments were held. The first had a front court with two towers projecting into it beside the main gate and within were the East and West Chōshuden Halls. A second gate led into a larger court with twelve more halls, four on each side and four in the middle. Lastly behind that was a third court with the Daikyoku Den or Grand Throne Hall, with a smaller one, the Shōanden, behind it. On the right and left of the Daikyoku Den were the towers of the Green Dragon and White Tiger. It was a building 22 yards square with a hipped roof covered with green tiles with kite-tail finials at each end of the ridge. The floor was also tiled and in the centre stood the Imperial Throne. The Daikyoku Den was burnt many times and was not rebuilt after the last fire in 1177. Recently a replica of it has been put up in Kyoto. The Chōdōin was set right in front of the Shujaku gate on the south-west of the palace. The Burakuin was 22 yards square and had a dais for the throne in the centre. In front and on each side were three smaller halls and behind it three more in a row on each side connected by colonnaded corridors. It was surrounded by a wall making an enclosure 112 yards east to west and 296 yards south to north. It was burnt and not rebuilt after 1063.

The ceremonies that had been performed in the Daikyoku Den were afterwards transferred to the Shishinden, the Front Hall of Audience in the palace itself. The palace had twelve gates as before and the Shishinden lay facing the Kenrei-mon or front gate across the courtyard. It is 90 feet east to west and 75 feet north to south. It has an inside corridor under the eaves and an inner chamber in the middle in which is the throne. The roof is of dressed rafters without a ceiling and on the north side are sliding screens painted with the figures of the great Chinese sages. It was burnt in 1227 and not rebuilt for a long time; the present structure dates from 1790. Restored exactly on the ancient model when the whole palace was rebuilt by the great Minister Matsudaira Sadanobu, the greatest pains were taken to get exact plans and information so that the style of the tenth century could be reproduced. After calling for tenders for the work Sadanobu accepted the highest one on the grounds that for fine construction a high price must be paid, and to consider anything else would show want of respect for the Court.

The actual residence of the Emperor was formerly the Jijuden, behind the Shishinden; but afterwards it was transferred to the Seiryoden which is a building of no great size—about 60 feet long by 30 feet wide. Inside is a main chamber which was the Imperial Living-room, one corner of it floored with earth on which it was necessary for His Majesty to stand when worshipping the Sun Goddess and other Deities. Next to this was the dining-room, the bed-chamber and an ante-room and behind this were the apartments for the Consorts. Adjacent were bathroom, dressing-room and lavatory, and at the back the kitchen and the entrance. The simple life of the Emperors of that time is very evident from these by no means elaborate arrangements.

It was in this age that the new dogma (probably invented in the preceding period by Gyōgi, but strongly advanced now by Kōbō and Dengyo) that Shinto gods were manifestations of Buddha in Japan began to produce what is called Ryōbu Shinto or Double-faced Shinto, that is to say a Shinto in which the gods become, as it were, adopted children of Buddha. This affected the architecture of the shrines which began to assume storied gates, pagodas, quadrangles, elaborate carvings and other appurtenances associated with Buddhism, while Buddhist monks often took charge of them—with the exception of the Ise shrine which never altered its ancient ways and where Buddhist monks were not even allowed to enter the precincts.

Though Hieizan was completely destroyed by Nobunaga in the late sixteenth century, Kōya San still survives as a specimen of these great groups of temples. It is very much like a Japanese equivalent of Oxford or Cambridge, though without any satellite residential town. Fish and women were rigidly excluded from Mount Koya up till 1870 and the latter are so still, though oddly enough liquor is not. But Hieizan was never so strict and it was not only monks that Nobunaga burnt. The great pagoda of Mount Koya was burnt in the nineteenth century, but some fifty temples remain, built with quadrangles with chapels and apartments for the many pilgrims who resorted there and special suites for the Imperial Envoys and feudal lords. In these apartments may be seen some of the finest speciments of Japanese interior decoration of the feudal age still actually in use. The mighty kitchens and bathrooms are interesting also, and the living-rooms contain a flue of plaster built over the hearth in the middle of the room to carry away the smoke or fumes—which I have neither seen nor heard of anywhere else in the country.

At the end of the long road that runs through the settlement is the mausoleum of Kōbō Daishi where, according to current belief, he sits in a long trance awaiting the coming of Maitreyya, the Buddhist Messiah. In front of it is a Hall of Lamps where lights burn perpetually; they have been dedicated by many famous people, and there is one that has never yet been extinguished since it was kindled by the Emperor Go-Shirakawa in the twelfth century, so it is said. Along the road has grown up a cemetery[3] where all the great of Japan have supernumerary tombs, thus assuring them the advantage of being in the van as usual when Kōbō rises. By the side of the Hall of Lamps is the Hall of Bones, a species of large letter-box in which the ashes of ordinary people may be deposited by their friends when they make the pilgrimage. The ashes are enclosed in a small earthen pot for the purpose. The roofs of the temple buildings here are covered with thick shingle like those of shrines, and certainly blend beautifully with the cryptomeria and other trees that surround them.

In the second part of this period, when the Fujiwara house held sway, architecture began to be assimilated to the national taste. By some these three centuries are divided into an early part from 900 to 1100, and a later from 1100 to 1192. But actually it was a gradual progress without definite lines of demarcation. In the temples a new phenomenon was the Amida Hall. With the end of the intercourse with T'ang and the comparative waning of the attractions of the esoteric sects, partly owing to strife which broke out among them, the easy-going cult of Amida Buddha began to make much more headway. It has been suggested that it is derived somehow from Christianity, as it has also been maintained that Kōbō's doctrine is a form of gnosticism. But there is no cogent evidence for either view and the natural tendencies of human nature seem sufficient to explain Amidism. Shingon promised enlightenment through ritual and gesture; but the Amida scriptures promised it through something much easier—just faith in Amida Buddha and repetition of the formula of appeal to

[3] This cemetery is a mile and a quarter long and must be unique. Few of the famous names in Japanese history since this time are lacking. Conspicuous is a monument to those who fell on both sides in Hideyoshi's Korean war "that they may attain enlightenment."

him. It promised something more attractive to the ordinary man than enlightenment, for it had a fine Paradise in the West (Saihō Jōdō, the Pure Western Land) to which believers would be fetched at death by Amida and his attendant Bodhisats riding on purple clouds of glory and playing on musical instruments. The paradise as depicted in art was evidently modelled on the Imperial Palace,[4] so the Fujiwara courtiers would naturally feel at home in it, and probably consider they had a prescriptive right to it from their support of temple funds, while it gave the ordinary man what such conceptions always do, the prospect of living in luxury without work. Amida was said even to have a boat of his own to transport the elect over the river of the underworld, thus saving them the fee placed in the mouth of all others for the infernal ferryman. There was nothing esoteric about all this; every one was welcome and was cordially invited by propaganda. So the temples became rather of a congregational type with an Amida Hall, containing only his image, and a large matted space where people could sit and listen to exhortations and descriptions of paradise out of the Amida texts. It is easy to see why it became the most popular sect with all classes, as it still is, though later on Zen supplanted it with the military caste. But this era was one in which they had not yet become important.

Another development of this period was the Shinden style of residence. It was that used by the Fujiwara courtiers and had developed from the Imperial Palace, which was an elaborate form of it. Shinden was the name of the principal chamber in the centre facing south, corresponding to the Shishinden of the palace.[5] On each side of this and connected by covered corridors were subsidiary buildings

---

[4] In the hell and paradise picture in the temple of Konkai-kōmyōji of the Kamakura period, the paradise is a really fine range of Shinden style two-story pavilions with a round pagoda at each end and three in the background. Some of the buildings are flat-roofed and single story. All are perfectly rectangular and have *shōji* on all sides. They suggest a somewhat etherialized Japanese edition of Hardwick Hall. They are situated on a large lake across which, but no doubt out of sight and hearing, hell flames rather reticently in a corner, hinting at comparatively infrequent use. This picture is now in the Kyoto Onshi Museum and is reproduced in Tsuda's *Handbook of Japanese Art*.

[5] Though differently spelt in Japanese, *shinden* means "sleeping chamber," and *Shishinden,* "purple imperial chamber." *Kayabuki* or reed thatch was preferred for the Shinden because it was the sleeping chamber and rain made no noise on it. The roofs were *irimoya* style.

called *tai* or "houses opposite." From these, two long covered ways at right angles enclosed the garden and extended to the lake in the middle of it, ending in an Izumi Dono and a Tsuri Dono—pavilions for cooling oneself and fishing respectively. In these covered ways were the "middle gates" for entry and exit. In the centre of the lake was an island with bridges connecting it with either bank. Behind the main buildings, and again connected with them by bridges and covered ways, were the rooms for the ladies and the family. A very good example of a large specimen of this type is the Kanin Detached Palace which was what was called a Sato Dairi or country palace where the Emperor could live outside the city, and where many were forced to live when the main palace was burnt in the military turmoils. The custom started when the Emperor Murakami in 961 went to live in the Reizeiin mansion after a fire. After another fire or so the Sovereigns found it pleasant to live outside in the mansions of the Regents and stayed there for years, so they decided to build Detached Palaces of their own, and the number of these increased till in time there were more than twenty of them.

The Byōdōin temple at Uji is an example of a residence of this time that has survived, for it was originally the villa of the Regent Fujiwara Yorimichi, which he afterwards turned into a temple. There were the usual subsidiary buildings, but they got burnt and the Hō-ō-do or Phoenix Hall, as it is called from the resemblance of its outline to this Imperial Bird, is the only part that is left (though the Hō-ō is hardly a phoenix). It is an excellent example of the way in which the Fujiwara nobles planned to ensure good fortune in this world and the next. The nobles were most assiduous in building big temples—an example the Emperors and Retired Emperors and their Consorts all imitated, so Michinaga's Hoshōji and Yorimichi's Byōdōin were followed by the six *shōji* built by the Emperors Shirakawa, Toba, Sutoku and Konoe and the Dowager Empress Taikenmonin, in which the influence of the palace style on that of the temple is very apparent.

The size of a noble's mansion was limited to one *bō*, i.e. 400 feet square. The Kanin palace is 840 north to south and 400 east to west. It was the largest of the country palaces. The size of the Shinden[6] or

---

[6] Prince Genji's Shinden was 70 feet square, the largest kind; many were about 50 feet.

main chamber of a residence varied from 72 feet square to 42 and 30.[7] *Shitomi* or wooden gratings such as are still seen in Shinto shrines, with the upper half hinged at the top to open outwards, were used to close in the outside when necessary, though these were not allowed in the houses of ordinary folk. Inside were curtains and screens to divide the rooms, and there were mats here and there on the boarded floor for the great ones to sit on. Ordinary houses had wooden doors and only a main building without extensions or pavilions. All were very largely open to the air like roofed verandas, and the modern Japanese house is very little different. What has been added is the result of the Zen architecture of the next period plus the extension of the use of mats in town houses. But a Japanese of the present day could live in one of these houses of the tenth century without any discomfort. These were the residences in which the authoresses Murasaki and Sei Shonagon lived and in which Prince Genji and his friends spent their elegant existences. The Regent Michinaga was famous for the mansion he built at Kyōgoku and the others strove to emulate the grandeur of this most splendid of the Fujiwaras. But all this had no effect on the ways of the common people who continued for long to live in small and primitive thatched huts and cottages.

The interior decorations of this period as we see them where they have survived in the Hō-ō-do at Uji and in the Chusonji at Hiraizumi are very brilliant, all the wall space and pillars being painted and lacquered in gold and colours over wood and stucco, or inlaid with mother-of-pearl with ornaments of ivory and enamel. By this time the art of lacquering had advanced very far and fine work could be done in gold and various colours. Of the pillars, some are round with entasis and others square with bevelled corners, the bevel being about a fifth of the width of the pillar. The arched windows in the Hō-ō-do are of the Kamakura period and were evidently added afterwards.

---

[7] Fujiwara Sadaie, the eminent poet, says in his diary (1226) that the land on which he was building his new house was 35 by 95 feet, and he was then Mimbu-kyo or Minister for Home Affairs of the Upper Third Court Rank. Sei Shonagon remarks in the *Makura-no-zōshi* that it does not look well to see such and such a Taiyu or Gon-no-kami living in a small board-roofed house with a new wooden fence of *enoki,* his ox-car drawn up in a cart-shed, a lot of trees close in front of the house, and the oxen tied up to eat the grass. Which shows that many did live in this rustic fashion.

Some of the frog-crotch struts in these buildings are of quite a different shape from those of the previous periods, though the older solid one is still found. The new type justifies its name much better for it is high and hollow and in some cases made of two pieces of wood joined in the middle. Those of the Chusonji, of this type, are covered with gold leaf over lacquer so that it is not possible to say whether they are one piece or two. Again, some of them have a little carving inside and it is from this kind that the extremely elaborate carved ones of the later periods developed. The roofs are hipped or hipped gable (*irimoya*) and the kite-tail finial is no longer found. For some time it seems to have been confined to the buildings in the Imperial Enclosure and now the "devil-headed" tile (*oni-gawara*) takes its place. This is an acroterion with a grotesque face in relief on it; but when flat and without this decoration it is still called "devil-plate" finial, as the place where the devil ought to be.

The Chusonji at Hiraizumi is a remarkable survival from the great temple built by Fujiwara Kiyohira in 1094. He and his son and grandson, Motohira and Hidehira, built and maintained the provincial capital of this northern province on the same lines as the real one. They were a branch of this courtier family who had become Lords of the Marches against the barbarian Emishi and so had specialized in militarism. Its two temples, the Chusonji and the Mōetsuji, were among the finest in the land, the former being an imitation of the *shōji* temples of Kyoto. There were others in the manner of the Byōdōin and the Sanjusangendo at Kyoto, and there were shrines like those of Gion and Fushimi Inari. Groves of cherry-trees were planted to look like Higashiyama and in the middle of it all stood the mansion of Hidehira.

The Chusonji had some forty buildings altogether, but all that is left is this brilliantly decorated Kondo and the library. The Kondo is an Amida Hall and in the centre of it the Buddha sits under the golden splendour of his canopy and the great pillars that support the 50-foot-high roof. All the beams and brackets are inlaid with mother-of-pearl and the metal mounts with cloisonné work. This building is an important one in another sense, in that it is the mausoleum shrine of the three generations of Fujiwara lords whose ashes are deposited under the altar; and from this idea in time developed the imposing mausolea of the Tokugawa Shoguns in the Edo period. But the actual plan of these, known as Gongen-zukuri, named after the "old Gongen" Ieyasu, originated in the Kaisando of Founder's Hall of the Eihōji temple of the Zen sect of the Muromachi period.

The five-storied pagoda of the Daigōji, finished in 936, is an interesting survival of this period, too, with the Hokkedo and Saihōdō of the same temple. It is 78 feet 4 inches high and the *sōrin* is 41 feet, rather more than a third of the height of the whole and more than half that of the body, making it the tallest spire on any pagoda. The interior of the lower story, ceiling, walls and pillars is profusely decorated with pictures of Bodhisattvas and vine-leaf and lotus blossom designs, shading off from one colour to the other (*bokashi*).

No doubt the pagodas of the Yakushiji and the Toshōdaiji and other temples were similarly decorated, while the later example of the Hō-ō-do shows a further maturity. The Fukiji and Hakusui are specimens of the Amida-do of this period. The former has the boat-shaped elbow bracket of the Asuka age, which still sometimes persists, and a coffered ceiling above the Naijin or sanctuary. It has a pyramidal roof with a nectar-pot and jewel on the summit.

CHAPTER VII

KAMAKURA PERIOD (1190-1340)

In the Kamakura era there was a renewal of the intercourse with China that had been interrupted in the later years of the T'ang period and several new sects of Buddhism were introduced. To the Six Sects of Nara and the two more esoteric sects of Heian were now added six more, Zen, Ji, Shin, Nichiren, Jōdō and Yuzu Nembutsu, and with them came new styles of architecture derived from the Sung dynasty that was then flourishing in China. These were the Tenjiku (Indian) and the Kara (Chinese), and in contradistinction from them the type that had grown up in the Fujiwara period was called Wa or Japanese. Actually these new styles were, like all other Buddhist architecture, of Indian origin modified in China, and the names have no special connexion with any particular details. Before long the Tenjiku merged into the Wa style and lost its individuality, and then the Kara mode combined with the Wa to form a new style that prevailed from the end of the Kamakura right on into the Muromachi period. Tenjiku was the style chosen by the famous monk Jōgen in which to rebuild the Great Buddha Hall of the Tōdaiji after it had been burnt by Taira Shigehira in the Gempei wars; but, largely because it was thus started in Yamato where the Wa style was very popular, it was soon absorbed by this latter.

The Kara style especially associated with Zen, however, was introduced into Kyoto and Kamakura; and since the Zen sect was soon adopted by the dominant military caste as particularly suited to their spiritual needs, its characteristic architecture also held its own and had considerable influence on the buildings of succeeding ages.

It must be remembered that this was the period when the new military dictatorship of Japan was inaugurated under Minamoto Yoritomo, who, after vanquishing the other great military clan of the Taira (that had held sway for the previous thirty years) obtained from the Emperor an edict making over the administration of the whole country to him as Shogun or Commander-in-Chief. This office became hereditary in his family, the Minamoto, and remained so till 1868.

The first great Zen temples of the Kara style in Kyoto founded by the monks Eisai and Dōgen were the Nanzenji and the Daitokuji. Then came the Five Temples, first in Kyoto, and then a second edition in Kamakura, the military capital that Yoritomo set up in the east. These were the Tenryuji, Sōkokuji, Kenninji, Tōfukuji and Manjuji in Kyoto and the Kenchoji, Engakuji, Jūfukuji, Jōchiji and Jōmyoji in Kamakura.

These Zen temples were quite different both in plan and detail from what had preceded them. Entering from the south there is the Sammon[1] or Great Two-storied Gate, then the Butsuden or Buddha Hall, the Hatto or Doctrine Hall and the Hōjō or Residence, all in one straight line on the axis of the gate, while on the left and right inside the gate, in place of the two pagodas of the Nara age, were the Tōsu or latrines and the Yokushitsu or bath house. The library and bell-tower and Zendo or Meditation Hall were also located on each side as convenient. Often there was a lotus pool with a stone bridge over it outside the Sammon and a front gate (Sōmon) before that. As far as the regular plan went it was like a return to the Shitennōji style, but the details were quite different. The pillars sometimes had a stone base on the foundation stones and the floor was of square stone slabs laid diagonally. The pillars were tapered at the top and bottom (the form called *chimaki*, an elongated rice-cake narrower at the ends). They were the same shape in the Tenjiku style too, but here the taper was only at the top, though occasionally there are exceptions. The brackets are more sharply curved also. Then instead of frog-crotches or struts, clusters of brackets are used to support the beams between pillars, these clusters being in some cases almost continuous. This arrangement is called *tsume-gumi* or close-bracketing. Ornamental brackets and capitals are also used in this style. Another characteristic is the spreading of the rafters like a fan in the upper story of a two-story building and elsewhere. The projecting ends of

---

[1] *Sammon* does not mean "three gates," but is for *San-gedatsu-mon,* "gate of the three liberations," (*Vimokchas*), by which one enters Nirvana. Upstairs it it has figures of Buddha and his sixteen Apostles.

the rafters at the corners are bevelled or tapered and not cut straight as before.

The ornamental window (*kato-mado*, flower-headed, or sometimes flame-headed, window) with an ogival top is first found in this period, and the top of the doors is also sometimes of this shape. It is of Indian origin, like all the rest of these details, and appears in China under the Sungs.[2] It is the pipal or lotus-headed window as found, for example, at Ajanta. There is also a new kind of curved tie-beam called lobster tie-beam (*ebi kōryō*). The ceilings are not coffered in the sanctuary, but flat, and no coloured decoration is found as a rule. Most of these buildings have two-storied roofs and the bracketing is very profuse and complicated.

It is unfortunate that, though, through the importance of Zen Buddhism, the Kara style has had such a great influence on Japanese architecture, the Shariden or Relic Hall of the Engakuji is the only contemporary specimen left. As it persisted, however, later structures serve to illustrate its details.

In the Tenjiku style there are also certain peculiarities. The brackets have a round base like the *saruto* of the Asuka period, but of a different shape, and they also go through the pillars and project each side (*sashi-hijiki*). This arrangement allows the much deeper eaves to be supported more efficiently, for the long brackets are cantilevered on to beams inside the pillars. Here the ends of the rafters are not pointed or bevelled as in the Kara style, but blunt. There is also a new form of strut or king-post called *o-heisoku* or "big jar strut" from its shape. It is found in both these styles, more often in the Kara; but in the Tenjiku it is more cylindrical and should perhaps be called "round strut."

The famous Shariden of the Engakuji is all that is left of that temple, built by the Regent Hōjō Tokimune in 1283. It was made to house a relic presented by the Shogun Sanetomo, so it is said, and may have been later than the other buildings of the temple. It stands on a stone stylobate and the pillars have bases. It is 35 feet square and also 35 feet high. The bracketing of the lower story is simple enough,

---

[2] There is a work preserved in the Tōfukuji called Tai Sung Shosanzu or Pictures of the Temples of the Sung Dynasty, illustrating most of these details from Chinese sources. It was probably brought from China for the architects' guidance.

but that of the upper is rather complex, with close-bracketing on the plates that lie on the tops of the pillars. It has "fist nosing" at the end of these plates and the doors are of Chinese panelled style (*san-karado*) swinging on a pivot and not on hinges. The doors and windows have arched heads and the latter wooden lattices. The verge boards of the gable ends are also a new form called "double verges." The tie-beam used here is also different from those inside the building. It has an "eyebrow" on the lower edge and a "sleeve cutting" on both sides.

A new variety of building in the Kara style is the Founder's Hall (Kaisando) of the Eihōji temple at Toyooka village of the Kani district of Gifu prefecture. It was not built till 1352, apparently, and so does not come strictly into the Kamakura period, but it comes before the South and North dynasties were united, and this interval is sometimes reckoned as in the Kamakura rather than in the Muromachi period. It is a double structure arranged with an inner sanctuary and a prayer hall in front of it, the two connected by an ante-chamber. The front portion has a single roof and is with the ante-chamber on a lower level than the inner, which is reached by two steps. It has the complicated detail of the Kara style with close-bracketing of the triple type, whereas the inner sanctuary has a single roof of simple design with only one bracket in the centre of the plate beside those over the four pillars. The roofs are of the hipped gable kind and of shingle, and they practically meet over the roof of the ante-chamber beneath, which is gabled. The whole arrangement and proportions of the shrine are very harmonious. If it were built with gable roofs it would be in the manner of the Hachiman shrine at Usa, but it is a much finer piece of work. It may owe something to this type but the plan was evidently an invention of this age and is, as before observed, the origin of the Gongen shrine. It is very pure Kara style and has elaborate ornamentation in the gable ends with a special type of verge-board and king-post on the tie-beams. The curve of the roofs of each part of the building is different.

Turning to the Tenjiku style, the Nandaimon or Great South Gate of the Tōdaiji at Nara is a well-known example. It was rebuilt by the priest Shunjōbō Jōgen in 1199, with the Great Buddha Hall; but the latter was again burnt by Matsunaga Hisahide in the Oda period and so does not survive in its original state. It is 120 feet wide by

90 feet high with three gates 15 feet wide and 20 feet high—a huge and imposing structure with its mighty pillars each made of one great tree, and its forest of bracketing. The brackets are mortised right through these pillars and project in sextuple form some 15 feet to support the eaves in front, though they do not extend horizontally. They are cantilevered on to the cross-beams that hold the pillars together, as can be seen in the illustration (Plate 71). The bracket capitals have a moulded base of the *sarato* type. These capitals are placed so that the corner elbow goes across them diagonally, which is characteristic of this style. This gate has no ceiling and the pillars are visible right up to their tops. On these tops are great capitals on which the cross-beams rest, and on these are the frog-crotches of the Tenjiku style supporting a second set of tie-beams on which rest the supports of the roof.

The library of Kami Daigo is another specimen. It is a pyramidal building with the roof sloping down in front to cover with its eaves a porch that has a colonnade of four pillars. There is no ceiling inside, but the Sutra library stands under a gabled roof of its own with finely proportioned doors, the pivots of which are inserted in a circular fluted fitting applied to the lintel and called *waraza* (straw seat). The sets of tie-beams resting on the tops of the pillars themselves support tapering struts that hold up the roof. The pillars of this building appear at first sight to have a bulge, but actually only the upper portion of them tapers. It is a very neat and well-mannered building of pleasing proportions.

The belfry of the Tōdaiji seems to date from 1239, for on the sixth day of the sixth month of that year it is written in the temple archives that the bell fell down and was hung again in the tenth month. This rebuilding in four months seems very rapid, but is not impossible. On the boss of the bell is the inscription "Cast on the thirtieth day of the ninth month of the first year of Enō (1239) by the chief bell-founder Sahyoe-no-jō Nobutoki and twenty craftsmen." The belfry has a hipped gable roof with a sharp curve. The bell is hung from a great log under which are solid frog-crotches that rest on two other logs of the same size and these again are supported in the same way on the transverse beams. These beams project through the pillars and have ornamental ends in the Tenjiku manner.

· 43 ·

THE COMPOSITE STYLE

The Main Hall of the Kanshinji temple at Kawakami in the Minami Kawachi district of Osaka is the stock example of the mixture of the Kara style with the Wa or Japanese. It is about 65 feet square by 45 feet high and has a hipped gable roof. On top of the pillars it has the three branched brackets of the Wa style and between them the double ones of the Kara. The pillars are round with tapering tops, but those supporting the lean-to roof of the porch are square.

A distinctly peculiar building in the Japanese style that is one of the sights of Kyoto is the Sanju-sangen-do, which belongs to this period. The name means the Thirty-three-ken Hall. It was originally built by the Retired Emperor Go-Shirakawa beside his palace of the Hōjuji-den, but was destroyed and rebuilt in 1267. Actually it is not 33 *ken* long but 35, just as the Temple of Seven Halls has not actually that number, nor the Sammon three gates. Just how it got the name is unknown; but anyhow it is the longest of all temples, its measurement being 384 feet 6 inches, though it is only 5 *ken* or 30 feet deep. This shape was intended to accommodate the thousand and more images that it contains, but it was also most convenient for the Samurai archers who got into the habit of using its veranda as a shooting-range—for which it is very well suited. Possibly the name may have come from the range. Whatever the monks may have thought of this indignity, it is not on record that they protested.

The following is a plan of the way the styles mingled.

It is to be noted that the frog-crotches of this age are already elaborately decorated with openwork carving and the triangular brackets of the tail rafters (*tabasami*) are also carved in various patterns. The shrines of this period continue to be more and more influenced by Buddhist architecture and now have pillars, bracketing and roofs just like those of temples. The curved Chinese gable over the porch (*kara-hafu*), which has been used ever since, now first made its appearance, it seems, for there are not, in Professor Amanuma's opinion, any unchallenged examples before these days. The Mikumari shrine at Akasaka village in the South Kawachi district of Osaka has three separate shrines set side by side and connected by a corridor, which is unusual. Another well-known example is the Itsukushima shrine at Miyajima, one of the Three Sights of Japan, and situated conveniently on the tourist route on its island in the Inland Sea. It is said to date from the Suiko era, but Taira Kiyomori rebuilt it on its present plan when he was Governor of that district and made it a place of Imperial Pilgrimage, because he thought the favour of its Deity was the cause of his greatness. But it was burnt in 1225 and rebuilt in 1242. Then Mori Motonari, Lord of Choshu, remodelled it in 1558, and the only part that has survived from the Kamakura age is the Kyakuden or Guest-God's Shrine. It is built in the Shinden style like a palace by the sea, which flows under part of it at high tide, and its shingled roofs blend harmoniously with the green hills in the background. Its layout is somewhat unconventional to suit the peculiar situation. The Guest Shrine has Sanctuary (Honden), Hall of Offerings (Heiden), and other buildings one behind the other like a temple, and its architecture is that of the Fujiwara period in all respects.

Not much is known of the palace architecture of this age, except that toward the end of it there was no proper palace and the Emperor lived in Sato Dairi or Rural Palaces. Yoritomo had rebuilt the palace in Kyoto, but it was burnt in 1219. It was partially rebuilt and burnt again in 1227. Then Go Daigo Tenno began to rebuild it; but his days were short and it was never finished. The Southern Emperor had various residences while the Northern Sovereign lived in the Tsuchi Mikado mansion in Nishi-no-Dōin. Other Rural Palaces were the Saga and Fushimi mansions, in the latter of which lived the Retired Emperor Go Saga and the Emperors Go Fukakusa and Kameyama.

As Japan was now under the control of military magnates, it was natural that a type of residence suitable to their needs should develop. Not all the details of it are clear, but generally speaking it was a simple kind of house with a board roof and floors on which sitting-cushions were used, and in some cases it was surrounded by a board fence and had earth-topped gates beside which were *yagura* or archers' towers for defence. The entrance was opposite the front gate and on the right was the *tozamurai* or apartment for the "outside retainers" who did not live in. On the left of the entrance was a wide veranda with a Chinese gable in the middle of it and an ordinary one at the end. The inner rooms had alcoves and shelves and a *shōin*,[3] a sort of reading alcove first found in this age and adopted from the Zen temple, and from which this kind of house came to be called Shōin style as distinguished from Shinden style, that of the court nobility. *Shōji* or papered sliding doors and wooden sliding doors were also used instead of the hinged *shitomi* of the Shinden mansion. There appears to have been a Spear Room, Head Inspection Room, Long Hearth Room, Reception Room, called Dei, Study, Official Document Room or Library (Kobunsho) and so on. Unlike the Shinden mansion it was all under one roof and not under several connected by corridors. But for lodging the retainers there may very likely have been other buildings.[4] Naturally no example of this kind of residence has survived; so what is known can only be deduced from descriptions in contemporary writings and to an extent from some plans of a later date, and quite possibly reproducing some later features such as the *tokonoma* and *chigaidana*, which were not yet known. There is, however, a reception room in the Kangakuin of the Enjōji temple at Otsu that has survived from this age. Grating windows were used in this period with wooden bars just like those in medieval Europe. They often formed a long continuous opening like a *ramma* (openwork frieze) above the ogee arched windows. These military residences were much like large farm-houses. The expression *Kita-no-kata* or Lady of the North for the wives of nobles or *Kita-no-Mandōkoro* (Government of the North) for those of Regents or Shoguns refers to the inner part of the house in which they lived, since these residences normally faced south.

---

[3] The Shōin was previously called Kaisho or reception room. Next to it was the Tonomo or hall where the Uchi-samurai or house-retainers lived. It was boarded, but with some *tatami*. The other guards who were not allowed inside, but lived by the gate, were called Tō-samurai (remote retainers).

[4] In the military mansion the Daimyo slept in the *hisashi* or veranda, the Samurai in the middle gate, and lower servants in the stable.

CHAPTER VIII

MUROMACHI PERIOD (1340-1570)

THE Muromachi period may be taken as from 1340 to 1570 or from the union of the North and South dynasties in 1394 to the end of the Genki era in 1573, about 230 years in the first case or 180 in the second.

No great innovation in architectural style took place in it, but the Kara style increased its popularity with that of the Zen sect and made its effects felt in other buildings beside temples. The other styles are found as well, however; but no very great architectural master-piece has survived from this age, in which the examples of the Kara style are inferior to those of the preceding one. Again, unfortunately more than half of the temples in Kyoto, the capital of the Ashikaga Shoguns who removed it back again from Kamakura, were destroyed in the civil wars of the Onin period (1460-). Architecture ran to elegance and delicacy rather than to grandeur—in which it was very representative of the age and the rulers, for the Ashikaga Shoguns were, with the exception of the first, luxurious and fastidious aesthetes who became more and more involved in the bonds of ceremony and convention. Consequently the Empire was never properly under their control and eventually they lost the little power they had and those feudal wars ensued which were so damaging to buildings.

The most prominent works of the period are residences rather than temples, for it became the fashion to build fine mansions in carefully planned landscape gardens, and the characteristic Japanese arts of garden-planning, tea-ism and flower arrangement as we know them, now arose under the Ashikagas to vigorous growth, though the germ had been there for a long time.

There is a big stupa-shaped pagoda at the Dai-dempōin at Negoro, the branch monastery of the Shingon monks of Mount Koya, rebuilt in 1516, that luckily survived Hideyoshi's burning of some of

the buildings in 1586. It is the largest specimen of this type and must
be much like the original at Koya which now no longer exists.

Also in the village of Bessho, in the Chiisagata district of Nagano
at the Anrakuji temple, is the only remaining example of an octagonal
pagoda in Japan. This is the common form in China, and small ones
of stone are to be seen in Japan too. There was a nine-storied specimen
of very large dimensions at the Hoshōji temple at Kyoto according to
tradition, but it is there no longer. This one is three-storied, with
another set of eaves below that makes it look four-storied; or perhaps
it was intended to have four stories, as an exception to the rule that
pagodas have always an odd number of stories. For Japanese dislike
even asymmetry unalloyed. It is 40 feet high and the *sōrin* (spire) of
cast iron is 20 feet high. The first two stories are noticeably closer
to each other than those above them and Professor Amanuma observes
that this is rather a feature of Zen buildings The style is strongly
Kara with some modifications in the detail.

The Kinkaku of the Kaenji, or Golden Pavilion, which is so well
known as to be a bit hackneyed, was begun in 1398 by the Shogun
Ashikaga Yoshimitsu on the site of a villa belonging to the Saionji
lord of that day, Kintsune by name. It was called the North Hill
Mansion (Kitayama Dono); but after his death he left it to be turned
into a temple. This Golden Pavilion is the only survivor of many
buildings which have all disappeared. It is a blend of residence and
temple. This three-storied pavilion in a landscape garden is a new
form of palatial residence produced by the ways of the age.

Yoshimitsu's villa had thirteen buildings in all. The Shishinden,
an imitation of that in the Imperial Palace, which was definitely pre-
sumptuous for a subject, the Hall of the Court Nobles, the Pavilion
of the Mirror of Heaven (Tenkyo-kaku), the Hall of the Confession
of the Doctrine (Gehōdo), the North-Gazing Hall (Kyōboku-do), the
Snow-Viewing Arbour (Kansetsu-tei), the Relic Hall (Shariden),
the Hall of the Waters (Izumi-dono), the Hall of Fragrant Virtue
(Hōtokuden), the Lesser Hall (Komi-do), the Jizo Hall (Jizo-do),
and others beside an arched bridge (Sori-bashi). The Shishinden was
of the eight-gabled type that originated in the Kamakura era with a
throne in the middle and eight dragons in gold lacquer on the roof,
if the descriptions are to be credited. The Kinkaku itself was
originally on an island in the lake and approached by the large arched

bridge from the Hall of Fragrant Virtue, as seems very suitable. The Ginkaku had twelve buildings, among them a Hall of the Waters called Pure Diversion Arbour (Rōsei-tei), a room constructed on a boat on the lake called Night-moored Ship (Yōhaku-sen), a roofed bridge called Dragon's Back Bridge (Ryūse-kyo), besides a Great Shōin, an Entrance Hall, and, not least, a bathroom.

The room on a boat is a device sometimes seen in modern residences and restaurants, and a very pleasing one in hot weather. Sometimes there is no lake but only one of those skilfully arranged groupings of rocks and water-plants that produce a vivid illusion of one.

When these Shoguns retired from the cares of office, such as it was, and which they were not slow to quit, they became Zen monks after the style of Retired Emperors, and since they lived in the Imperial Capital and not a military one like the lords of Kamakura or Edo, the imitation was the more natural. Actually their dress and the ecclesiastical touches in the architecture of their mansions were about the only monastic aspects of their life.

The first two stories of the Kinkaku are the same size, 30 feet by 24 feet, and there is a porch projecting from the ground floor. They are called Hōsui-in (Hall of the Water of Doctrine) and Chōōn-kaku (Pavilion of the Sound of the Tide) respectively. The third story, called Kyukeicho (Carefully-finished Top), is about 18 feet square and has a pyramidal roof with a nectar-pot finial on which is a jewel-shaped boss surmounted by a phoenix of gilt bronze. The two lower stories are in the Wa (Japanese) style with *shitomi* lattices and Chinese pivoted doors (*ita-karado*). Both have verandas round them and outer balconies, that on the second story being supported by bracketing. The upper story has Chinese panelled doors (*San-Karado*) with ogee arch windows and lotus ornamented balcony rail in Kara style. The two lower stories were decorated in colours over black lacquer while the third was covered with gold leaf both within and without, hence the name given to the whole. Professor Amanuma gives the proportions of the first and second stories as, Wa style 7/10, Kara 1/5, Tenjiku 1/10; and of the upper story as Kara 9/10. The effect of this pavilion is somewhat reminiscent of Akbar's marble Panch Mahall at Fatehpur Sikri, though this is a three- and not a five-storied Vihara.

The Ginkaku or Silver Pavilion of the Gishōji is of the same kind but smaller and two-storied, while its details conform to the Shōin style rather than the Shinden. It also is the only survivor of much more extensive establishment, for Ashikaga Yoshimasa began to build himself a villa here when the Onin war of 1468 interrupted his operations, and it was not till 1480 that he took up his residence again after his retirement and resumed them; but the building was not finished when he died seven years after.

The lower story is 23 by 18 feet and the upper is 18 feet square, very modest dimensions indeed. The roof is like that of the Kinkaku and the intention was to finish it with a covering of silver leaf, but this was never done and it is silver only by courtesy. The style is much the same as the other too, but the lower story has a flat boarded ceiling and waist-high *shōji* (*kōshi-shōji*) with sliding wooden doors, approaching very nearly to the modern Japanese interior. The upper story has three arched windows in front and two, with a pair of panelled doors, on the opposite side; this is repeated on the two other sides.

Attached to the same temple of Gishōji is the Tōkyudo, Yoshimasa's private Buddhist chapel with a tea-room of four and a half mats, the first to be constructed in Japan.[1] It measures 30 by 24 feet and is 22 feet high, with a shingled hipped gable roof and a veranda round it. This also has waist-high *shōji* and boarded floor. The Buddhist shrine of Amida has a coved ceiling and Chinese panelled doors on pivots with a board floor, while the tea-room floor is covered with the four mats and a half that was to become the normal size for this kind of chamber. It has a board ceiling, a built-out writing alcove (*tsuke-shōin*), and a chigaidana or set of shelves. Here too there are waist-high *shōji* and *mairado* or ribbed wooden sliding doors.

The shrines of the Muromachi era again became more and more like Buddhist temples with double hipped gable roofs and elaborate carvings, so that it is very difficult at times to distinguish between the two. The Kibitsu shrine at Ichinomiya in the Kibi district of Bizen province is an ancient one said to date from the days of the Emperor

---

[1] I have not included any plans or details of tea-rooms and their construction in this volume since they have already been dealt with in my work *Chanoyu*. There are excellent photographs of them in Harada's *Lesson of Japanese Architecture*, Yoshida's *Das Japanisches Wohnhaus*, and Tamura's *Landscape Gardens*.

Nintoku, A.D. 313; but the present structure was rebuilt by Ashikaga Yoshimitsu in 1390 and is a very complicated building. The roof is shingled and has double gables over the hip of the *irimoya*, while the oratory or Haiden is built on in front like a vestibule. Inside the floor rises in stages and the ceiling with it, which gives a somewhat uncommon effect. The pillars carry *sashi-hijiki* or traversing brackets in the Tenjiku style. The oratory is also two-storied, but the lower story has a tiled roof like that of a veranda and over this a range of lattice windows, a feature very rarely found. It has also the "lobster" tie-beams and jar-shaped king-posts of the Kara style. The outside of the roof has the typical Shinto cross-beam construction, but only applied and loosely connected with the ridge, looking like an afterthought.

This age was not an auspicious one for the Imperial Palace and its occupants. It was burnt several times and the Northern Emperor set up by the Ashikaga Shogun lived in the Tsuchi-mikado Detached Palace. It was burnt in the Onin civil wars and the Emperor escaped the fire with difficulty. Then, in 1478, attempts were made to rebuild it on a much smaller scale, but the country was distracted by feudal wars and the Imperial Domains were lost so that the Throne had no funds and had to depend on contributions from some loyal feudal lords. The great Court festivals could no longer be observed, for there were no proper buildings in which to hold them. Even the Senyōden where the Sacred Mirror was kept was in ruins.

The feudal lords, however, like the Shogun, had a tradition of magnificence, and in the latter days of the Ashikaga house the great lords were more wealthy and secure than the Shogun. None of their mansions have survived, but the descriptions of the Flower Palace of Yoshimitsu at Muromachi show that it was a mixture of Shōin and Shinden styles, a blending of the Court style with the military residence. It had an entrance hall, Shinden and Shōin halls and *tai* or connected wings. But the mansions of Yoshimasa and Yoshinao were entirely in the Shōin style.

The word *shōin* means "study" and it was taken from the architecture of the Zen temple imported from India via China. In the temple it was the name of the library, for it literally means writing or book room; but when the military class became so much given to Zen they made such a room in their residences, where they could read

Chinese texts (for the Zen monks taught the Confucian classics also) or meditate if so inclined. And as they came to receive guests there the reception room acquired the name Shōin. The inner part of it was raised as a dais (*jōdan* or upper step) on which the lord sat. Behind this was the *tokonoma* or alcove and the *chigaidana* or asymmetric shelves, a variety of built-in sideboard. The rooms were divided from one another by *fusuma* and closed in on the outside by *shōji*; but *amado*, or outside wooden rain-doors sliding on the edge of the veranda, were not introduced till the Momoyama age and then were not universal.

The word *genkan* or entrance hall (dark space) was another expression borrowed from the Zen monastery and is now the ordinary word for this part of a Japanese house, while in these days the word *shōin* is still used to mean the built-in writing table with small *shōji* behind it, which is often found beside the *tokonoma* in reception rooms of the better kind. The decoration of the interior of these rooms was confined to black-and-white sketches on the walls and *fusuma*. The wood was plain but might be lacquered black in some cases.

After the Genkan or porch was attached to the house the chamber within was enlarged and became the place where the Samurai retainers hung up their weapons and which they used as a guard-room. So its name became changed from Hiro-hisashi (wide veranda) of the Shinden style to Hiroma or Great Hall of the Shōin, and the Tozamurai of the older military residence was no longer needed or provided.

The Ashikaga house had *shitomi* and *yarido* (suspended grating windows and sliding doors) and a Tozamurai (guard-house). The floors were all boarded and had loose *tatami* (mats) that were moved about where they were needed; but the floors were not yet covered entirely with them.

In the temple buildings there is a great increase of carving everywhere, on the beam-ends, frog-crotches, verges and openwork friezes over the lintels (*ramma*). And the bracket capitals, too, become ornamented and foliate—the beginning of the debased forms they assumed in later days. On the other hand the influence of the Zen simplicity had banished the red and other coloured decoration, and plain wood became the rule both inside and out.

Kō-no-Moronao (d. 1351) said that ordinary Samurai below the fourth rank should not have boarded roofs of the kind called *seki-ita-uchi*, or even *noshi-buki*. They must have ordinary thatched roofs like those of farm-houses. The first kind is the more elaborate, made of overlapping boards with longitudinal braces to keep them in place; and the *noshi* roof is made of layers of thin boards held down by diagonal cross-pieces over which stones are laid to prevent the wind dislodging them. These roofs are common in the Hokuriku district in the north still.

The Daimyo Otomo in the fifteenth century lived in a thatched house with no *tatami*. If all lords had been like him the land would have been at peace, observes the chronicle.

In the Muromachi period even Samurai did not have a house with a large Shōin style room, much less the ordinary people. And most of the floors were of boards without *tatami*. The large boarded spaces in farm-houses are a survival of this. They are like those in the refectory of a temple.

The *tokonoma*, now a deep alcove in which pictures or scrolls of writing are hung and flower arrangements placed, always found in a reception room and in tea-rooms also, probably developed out of the Zen shrine which consisted of a picture of Buddha or Daruma hung on the wall with a small oblong table standing before it to hold a candlestick, flower vase and censer. This table was called *oshi-ita* and was used in rooms of the Ashikaga time, but when it became a fixture it developed into the *tokonoma*. Even now a detachable stand of this kind is used in rooms that are too small for a normal *tokonoma*, the size of which must be in proportion to that of the room.

The *chigaidana* was probably a built-in version of the cabinet with similar shelves used in the Fujiwara Shinden mansion, though some say that these shelves were first used in the military residence and were put there for the heads taken by the warrior, the different levels in this case being explained as intended to correspond with the rank of the deceased and pay proper respect where it was due.

CHAPTER IX

MOMOYAMA PERIOD (1570-1616)

THE Momoyama period is a short one of only forty years or so; but for activity it has been described as one in which every decade was equal to a century in most others, and as usual its architecture reflected its exceedingly vigorous life. This era saw the country united under one central administration by Nobunaga and Hideyoshi, those two remarkable characters who brought out of confusion and civil wars the beginning of the modern Japanese Empire. But, though rulers, they could not become Shogun, for neither happened to be of the Minamoto family from which alone convention decreed that Shoguns could be taken. Hideyoshi indeed was of no family at all. Nobunaga was one of the few Japanese autocrats to be assassinated when a little under fifty, and Hideyoshi died in 1598, whereupon their work was carried on by a third even more remarkable figure who was a Minamoto and therefore could and did become Shogun and the Divine Ancestor of a line of fifteen successors in that office. Though the Momoyama period actually ceased at the fall of the Toyotomis, the family of Hideyoshi, its atmosphere in architectural matters extended right on into the next period of the Tokugawa Shoguns, more or less till the end of the seventeenth century.

The speciality of this age was not so much religious edifices as palatial residences, military mansions and castles, or perhaps the *simplex munditiis* of tea-rooms. As in the previous years the Wa, Kara, Tenjiku and Composite styles continued to flourish and in details grew rather more ornate than ever. But though this was so the adventurous spirit of the time led it to the limit in experiments within these boundaries. And these experiments lay mostly in the sphere of painted and carved decoration of every sort, for great strides had been made in these arts of late and there were many great artists, craftsmen and aesthetes ready to serve these brilliant and stimulating autocrats, of whom the first two, Nobunaga and Hideyoshi, were themselves exceedingly enthusiastic connoisseurs of all that was beautiful and uncommon. This is well seen in the two palatial mansions that they built, the Azuchi castle of Nobunaga and the Fushimi-Momoyama castle of Hideyoshi from which the period is named, not to mention Hideyoshi's Juraku mansion in Kyoto and his castle of Osaka. A bit vulgar and blatant it all may have seemed to the more subdued taste of the century before, but its colourful vigour was natural and characteristic, especially of a parvenu like Hideyoshi. For though some of the details were overloaded and some of the ornament useless, the architecture remained on the whole healthy, and real degeneration did not set in until the later period of Edo.

It was hardly to be expected that temple building would flourish under Nobunaga, for he hated the political activities of such sects as the Monto Amida Buddhists and Nichiren monks, which were rather pronounced in his day. And what Nobunaga disliked he had a habit of burning if he could. So that the destruction of religious buildings and their occupants under his rule was considerable. He saw in them an obstacle to his plan of establishing a central government for Japan. So did Hideyoshi in some cases, but he has been described as one whose speciality was water rather than fire and he preferred to flood out his enemies, a process that was not so destructive. Hideyoshi was by nature far the less drastic of the two and preferred to use temples for advertising himself, creating employment and popularity and making other people spend money.

Another phenomenon peculiar to this age was the appearance of Christian edifices like the colleges at Azuchi and Arima—groups of buildings in the Spanish or Italian style with chapel and campanile complete, as can be seen from the one or two rare illustrations that have survived. There was a big church in Kyoto called the Eirokuji or Temple of the Eiroku Era, from the date of its construction, but apparently better known to everybody as the Nambanji or Temple of the Southern Barbarians. The interior is said to have been in European style, but some consider that the outside was not; and certainly a few rare screen pictures of the activities of the Portuguese at Nagasaki show what seem to be Christian churches in Japanese style, built like temples with a tower like a stupa pagoda, but with a cross on the top in place of the usual Buddhist finial. Oddly enough

Nobunaga encouraged all this, not out of any liking for Christianity itself, for he was a rationalist, but because he hoped to see the political variety of it damage the same kind of Buddhism. Partly, too, because the missionaries brought him novelties which he appreciated, and had knowledge he could acquire. So it flourished all his days, but after his untimely death in 1582 Hideyoshi became suspicious of the Europeans, and started those repressive measures which continued under the Tokugawas and ended in the closing of the country and the very thorough destruction of everything suggestive of Christianity, even to the use of the date A.D.

But Hideyoshi favoured Buddhism to the extent that he liked to use it to glorify himself as well as to assist him politically. Thus he determined to build the biggest Buddha ever known, 160 feet high, and a temple 200 feet high to house it. This was the Hōkōji, intended to put the Great Buddha Hall of Nara in the shade. It was built in 1587, but destroyed in the great earthquake of 1612 and rebuilt again by his son Hideyori, on a smaller scale, with a 63-foot Buddha and a 160-foot temple. This was again destroyed in another earthquake and fire in 1798, and the present edifice that takes its place beside the Toyokuni shrine of Hideyoshi is very small indeed. This temple had a strangely political career, for when Hideyoshi built it he ordered the people to contribute their weapons for its metal work, thus disarming them, and literally forging their arms into hinges for the doors of the temple of the peaceful one to turn on. After its destruction Tokugawa Ieyasu, even more cunning than Hideyoshi, persuaded his son Hideyori to spend any amount of money in rebuilding it so that he might not have the wherewithal to buy armaments. Finally, when it was rebuilt, Ieyasu, who had repudiated with indignation the suggestion that he should contribute something to it, made the inscription on its great bell a pretext to start a war with Hideyori and eventually destroy him. It was in some sort an epitome of the methods of those interesting times. The plan that has survived from about 1700 shows that it was just the same type as the Nara Daibutsu-den built in the Tenjiku style with septuple bracketing, the largest number used. It had 92 pillars from 5 to $5\frac{1}{2}$ feet in diameter, or, according to Amanuma, 88. It was supported by four huge tie-beams connecting the four pillars that surrounded the space where the image was placed, just like the 78-foot beams (13-*ken* beams) of the present-day Tōdaiji

Daibutsu-den. The dimensions given on the plan are 110 feet long by 70 feet deep.

The Kyō-ō Gōkokuji or Tōji is another building with a mixture of styles, for it has Tenjiku pillars and brackets with a Wa style quadrangle and bracketing in the upper story, while the shape of the brackets throughout is of the Wa type.

The kitchen and refectory (*Kuri*) of the Myōshinji is a fine specimen of the work of this age. Tradition says it was built by Hideyoshi when he fed a thousand monks, and the date 1605 is on the end tile of one of the gabled smoke-vents. It is 74 feet long by 78 feet deep and 51 feet high to the roof ridge. It has a Chinese gable over the entrance and all the details, frog-crotches, verges, tie-beams and beam-ends are elaborately carved, and the *omoto* or *Rhodea japonica* appears here as a decoration for the first time. There are two gabled smoke-vents on the high roof, the eaves of which roof come down to within 21 feet of the ground. One part of the interior is covered with mats and with the exception of the earthen part the rest is floored with boards. The ceiling is what is called *no-tenjo,* i.e. one that has the beams covered in with ordinary boards like an outhouse. As a temple refectory this one is certainly out of the ordinary.

The Kōdaiji was built by Kōdaiin the wife of Hideyoshi (posthumous name) as a mausoleum for him in 1606. The pillars and doors and other fittings are all finished in what is known as Kōdaiji lacquer and the ceilings of the Kaisando or Founder's Hall are made from the wood of a warship that Hideyoshi used in the Korean campaign and from his wife's palanquin. Some of the finest lacquer work of the time was designed by Hon-ami Kō-etsu and known by his name. Its merit lay in taste and design rather than any technique, and it is very often done on a background of plain wood. In the Kōdaiji is the tea-room that Hideyoshi used, and there is another in the Hiunkaku, his villa.

The Daigo Samboin at Yamashina is a temple that Hideyoshi restored to use for a flower-viewing festival. The buildings are a mixture of a Shinden with a tiled roof and a Shōin with a thatched one. The garden Hideyoshi designed himself, as he also supervised the restoration of the rooms, for which, as usual, he used material taken from other temples.

Two new forms of shrines appear about this time, namely the

Gongen type and a modification of it called the Eight-roofed style (Yatsu-mune-zukuri). The Gongen style derives from the Eihōji temple with its oratory and sanctuary joined by a connecting chamber. When this middle chamber is on the same level as the oratory it is called Heiden or Hall of Offerings, but when it is lower, as in the Eihōji, and paved with stone it is called the Stone Chamber (Ishi-no-ma) as it is at the Nikko Tōshōgu. Then two wings are pushed out from the oratory and a lean-to attached to the sanctuary, producing a fairly complicated roof called the Eight-roofed type, though the actual number is not so many. The only shrine that has its full complement is the well-known Tenjin shrine at Kitano in Kyoto, built in 1608— and that has really only seven. It is the first shrine to have a Stone Hall. It has a Chinese gable over the porch and a *chidori*[1] gable in the roof over it—which is quite superfluous and in poor taste, for it does nothing but look expensive. This shrine is a good example of the extent to which Shinto had been absorbed, externally, by Buddhist architecture.

The same thing happened to the Imperial Palaces which were again rebuilt first by Nobunaga and then by Hideyoshi and Ieyasu. The Shishinden and Seiryoden and Senyoden and the other buildings rose again, but with the original Shinden style was now mingled the Buddhist that was so pervasive. When they were again restored and largely reconstructed in the Kanei era (1624-41) by Tokugawa Iemitsu, several of the buildings were presented to various temples and re-erected, so that they can still be seen. One of these is the Imperial Envoy's Gate of the Daitokuji Zen monastery at Kyoto. It was once the south gate of the palace as rebuilt by Hideyoshi in 1591, and was transported here in 1641. It is largely in the Kara style, a very graceful though elaborately decorated structure. Part of the Katsura Detached Palace, a very famous building, is of this age also, for the Shōin and Gepparo pavilions were built by Hideyoshi for Prince Tomohito, adopted son of the Emperor Ogimachi. The rest of

---

[1] *Chidori* gable, or dormer. *Chidori* means "sea-gull" and the explanation is that this gable is three-cornered like a sea-gull. But Fujita thinks it a corruption of an old word *chidaru* which was the name of this dormer on a hipped roof to let out the smoke, instead of the small gable end of the hip in the irimoya. Afterwards the Chinese word *hafu* (wind-break) for a gable was introduced and the two were combined.

it and the garden were the work of Kobori Enshu when he was Commissioner for Fushimi. It is a very simple set of thatched buildings arranged *en échelon* from the Shōin to the Miyuki Goten and "looking when viewed from the garden rather like a house-boat." This view from the garden is most elegant and, though very simple, the villa has infinite variety in its construction and all the details are uncommon. Naturally it is much imbued with the Chanoyu feeling.[2]

The same process of removal to temples has fortunately preserved some splendid examples of mansions of the Momoyama age. There are the remains of Hideyoshi's Jurakutei mansion and the Hiunkaku lake villa now in the grounds of the Nishi Hongwanji monastery, where they were sent by Iemitsu, and the Great Shōin or Hall of Audience at the same temple with the No stage, the adjoining reception rooms and the Imperial Envoy's Gate (Chokushi-mon) all from his mansion at Fushimi. These represent the full flower of the Shōin style with dais at the upper end and a rather shallow *tokonoma*, the wall behind decorated with paintings on a ground of gold like the *fusuma* that divide the rooms, and the friezes (*ramma*) profusely carved in openwork. Beside the dais are four doors above a deep sill that is lacquered black like those of the dais and *tokonoma*. These doors open on to the Tonomo or Guard Chamber where the armed retainers stood unseen, ready for any emergency. They also are painted and have heavy tasselled cords to draw them back instead of the usual sunk pushes or *hikite* which are normally found. Next to it is the ante-chamber and then the third chamber divided off by painted *fusuma*. The rooms have *shōji* with *mairado* or wooden doors outside them. Beyond them is the wide matted veranda or corridor called *irikawa* and beyond that again the narrower wood-floored one. Later on *amado* or outside shutters were fitted on the outer edge of this, making the *mairado* unnecessary. The Great Gate, of the "four-legged" variety, (Yotsu-ashi-mon) is a massive and imposing structure most elaborately carved, though without impairing its constructive qualities or giving it the overloaded effect of the Nikko gates. More delicate and not so heavily ornate is the Karamon or Chinese Gate of the Daitokuji monastery that came from the Jūraku mansion. It is 30 feet high and 33 feet wide with Chinese gables on each side,

---

[2] Both Harada (*The Lesson of Japanese Architecture*) and Yoshida (*Das Japonisches Wohnhaus*) have fine photographs of it.

making it 25 feet deep. The gates have fine metal mounts, the beams are carved with fish in waves, dragons and lions, and the ends of the gables filled in with openwork carvings of birds and pine-trees.

The Great Hall of the Hongwanji is 207·3 feet long and 92·2 feet wide. It may be divided into two parts. The Great Hall of Audience, called Kō-no-ma or Crane Chamber because the *ramma* are carved with these birds with backgrounds of reeds and clouds, is said to be the work of Hidari Jingoro, the Grinling Gibbons of Japan. The *tokonoma* has a projecting Shōin with a large ornamental window, and the ceiling, which is a coved coffered one over the dais and a flat coffered one elsewhere, has paintings of birds and flowers, dragons and the like in the coffers. The *fusuma* and the walls and lower parts of the waist-high *shōji* are all painted with designs on a gold ground— Chinese scenes on the dais and flowers and birds elsewhere, mostly by Kano Tannyu. Behind the *tokonoma* is a scene with the Emperor Wu and the goddess Si Wang Mu which is characteristic, for these Japanese autocrats liked pictures of Chinese Court scenes, especially those of the great Empire of T'ang, just as Napoleon and others liked to recall ancient Rome. It is to be noted that the doors of the Tonomo here are in line with the *tokonoma* and not at right angles to it as else- where. Behind these spacious rooms is a smaller set called the White Shōin, also with dais reception room decorated in the same way with second and third chambers in front of it. The Dais Room has also a dressing-room in its rear. Parallel with these and the Great Reception Room on the left are another series of rooms, the Chrysanthemum and Wild-goose chambers with an *irikawa* and an ante-chamber, beside which is the entrance hall with another ante-chamber. On the right side is a third *irikawa* and three more rooms, the Drum Room (Taiko- no-ma) and the Wave Room (Nami-no-ma), named as usual from the subject of the decoration and as richly ornamented as the rest.

Hideyoshi's lake villa, the Hiunkaku or Flying Cloud Pavilion, rises in three stories of different sizes something like a very exagger- ated version of the Ginkakuji. The lower story has two main rooms: the reception room called Shokenden (Hall Inviting Discrimination) with dais and projecting Shōin windows; it is sometimes called the Willow Chamber because it is decorated with willows under snow by Kano Eitoku. Next to it is the ante-chamber and then the Embarking Chamber, with steps leading down to a landing stage from which to enter a boat. The second story has also Jōdan and Gedan, dais and lower room, and the papered ceiling of the Jōdan is decorated with paintings by Kano Sanraku, while there are also pictures of the Six Poets after which it is named. This story has a balcony round it. The third story, called Plucking Star Pavilion (Tekiseirō), is quite small and has ornamental windows shaped like a war fan. The roofs are all of shingle and comprise all shapes, hipped gable, Chinese gable, ordinary gable and pyramidal. The timbers with which is it built are all quite light and slender and unadorned, and its recherché but simple elegance shows the influence of the Chanoyu feeling very strongly, as might be expected of any one so devoted to it as Hideyoshi and such a friend of the first of Tea-masters, Sen Rikyu.

Attached to the Hiunkaku by a covered way is the bathroom, called Kikakudai[3] or Yellow Crane Terrace. It measures 66 by 24 feet, and consists of a single-storied building with a shingled pyramidal roof in which is a sitting-room with a balcony looking over the lake, attached to another on a lower level with a gabled roof for the dressing-room, next to which comes the bathroom itself on a lower level still. The bath is a steam chamber with a Chinese gabled roof, and the sitting-room is decorated with convolvulus by Kano Eitoku. The end of the sixteenth century was not, I imagine, except perhaps in India, Turkey or Cairo, a period when bathrooms, elegant or otherwise, were very common; so that this one, built as it is entirely of wood, is the more noteworthy. There is also a tea-room attached to the villa, which, it is perhaps unnecessary to say, is perfectly well suited in every way for modern living conditions.

Up to this time there had not been in Japan anything that could properly be called a castle. There were only hills and other strategic places defended by moats, natural or artificial, earthworks, and stockades. These were effective enough for their purpose, which was

---

[3] This may seem an odd name for a bathroom, but it is an auspicious one in Chinese classical circles, on account of the picture of a yellow crane which an impecunious tippler drew on the wall of a wine-shop to pay his account, assuring the host that it would dance if his customers sang and clapped their hands in time. So it proved, and the publican made a fortune out of the crowds who came to see it. Eventually the tippler came back and played the flute, whereupon the bird detached itself from the wall and carried him up to heaven on its back. A story that appealed strongly to the wine-loving and spendthrift literati of the T'ang period.

the protection of the lord's residence against sudden raids or the holding of an important place for a time by a garrison, as blockhouses on a provincial frontier. But the Japanese Samurai did not fancy the defensive much and usually preferred to use these forts as places from which he could sally out to the attack. The feudal lords depended on their field army and knew better than to be cooped up in places where it might be surrounded. And it was said of Takeda Shingen, one of the greatest strategists of the day, that he never built any strong place. This was partly, no doubt, because his provinces of Kai and Shinano were exceedingly mountainous and he could hold them very well as they were. And the nature of the country with its narrow roads and gorges between hills and its stretches of flooded ricefields on the flat, intersected only by narrow paths, meant that it was to a large extent a natural fortress and little more was needed. The strongest places were such sites as that of Osaka—which the Hongwanji monks held against Nobunaga for seven years, and even then they were only persuaded to get out by Imperial Edict. This was so surrounded by rivers as to form natural moats almost all round it, one of them being wide enough to make it easy to get provisions without interference from the besiegers.

However the introduction of firearms made it advisable, perhaps under the influence of European fortress plans, possibly supplied by the Portugese, to proceed to heavier fortifications and crenellated walls and towers. Firearms and Christianity entered Japan at almost the same time and in the same place, somewhere about 1540 and in the province of Satsuma in the island of Kyushu, the Daimiate of the house of Shimazu, the most ancient of the families of military aristocrats in Japan. Thus if, as some aver, the Jesuits gave Nobunaga the plans of the first castle, the antidote was supplied by the Portuguese as well as the poison—somewhat as they seem to have supplied the first public hospitals, after they had brought syphilis to fill them. They were, as a Japanese historian comments, then a very energetic people. But the Japanese themselves were no less so, for the castles they forthwith proceeded to build were extremely imposing looking piles, with their lofty many-gabled keeps rising story over story in the main ward and surrounded by heavily walled second and third wards with lofty towers and massive loopholed gates. They look bigger as a rule than their European prototypes and certainly handsomer, but they are not so consistently massively built, since their upper structures of walls and towers were made only of wood and plaster. The great ramparts beneath, however, lack nothing of solidity, and the moats were generally some 60 or 70 feet wide. But though they look formidable enough few of them were ever used, for they were built after the country had been unified and pacified by Hideyoshi and further consolidated by Ieyasu. Hideyori did sustain a siege in the greatest of them outside of Edo, the castle of Osaka, but it was taken more by intrigue than by assault, and practically all the fighting took place outside it. Therefore the historian Tokutomi is not far wrong in calling these castles "great advertisement towers," very typical of a flamboyant age that liked to make a fine show.

The first of these castles was built by Nobunaga in 1576[4] on Azuchi Hill, which projects into a lagoon formed by two islands between two long promontories, thus making it into a natural moat round the hill on three sides. Nothing of it now remains but the foundation stones, for it was burnt soon after its lord's death. It was a mixture of fortress and residence with a seven-storied keep called Tenshu, a word first found in this period, and first applied to the keep of a castle at Itami. It is equivalent to Teishakuten or the Heaven of Brahma, the highest of the thirty-three Heavens of Mount Sumeru, which according to Buddhist pictures rises in tiers like a huge wedding-cake, and has nothing to do with Christianity as sometimes alleged. This keep has its architectural prototype in the Kinkakuji and Ginkakuji pavilions of the Ashikagas, of which Hideyoshi's Hiunkaku is a further development. It was situated in the Hon Maru or main ward, the wards of a Japanese castle being called Kuruwa or Maru, both words meaning round. There were also Ni-no-maru and San-no-maru, second and third wards. Round the main castle were the fortified mansions of the great lords, his vassals and allies. The keep stood on a stone foundation 70 feet high and was of seven stories, rising over a 100 feet more.

---

[4] Castles began to be built in Japan when they were becoming disused in Europe. They were retained chiefly as strongholds to keep the country in order and the Shogun in power, since all the most important ones were in the hands of his relatives and vassals. They also involved the Daimyos in considerable expense for upkeep. Since the fortified part was not used as a residence they were not abandoned for greater comfort. No dungeons were ever associated with them and they have never been degraded by being converted into prisons.

Nobunaga's secretary has left a careful description of the interior which he says contained forty-five rooms and a landscape garden 72 feet long on the fourth story, with rocks and trees. On this story, too, was a place for playing hand-ball. The sixth story had an octagonal room with an area of 24 square feet of which the inner pillars were lacquered red and the outer ones gilt. One reception room was covered with linen lacquered black and another was all gilt without any other decoration at all, but very many were painted with such subjects as the Confucian sages, Buddha preaching to his disciples, Taoist Rishi and the more usual bird and flower, bamboo and pine motifs. It was "a splendid residence with superb views from the various apartments over the lake and its islands, to the distant hills beyond with the villages nestling in the plain between, and from the temple of Chōmyoji the sound of the evening bell came echoing over the water." A very suitable dwelling for a martial aesthete and at the same time a demonstration to the whole country that here, surrounded by the mighty, he ruled it.

It is said that the keep of Azuchi[5] was sharp at the top and looked like a Siamese pagoda, and it is suggested that this may have been due to a Portuguese strain introduced by Nobunaga's missionary acquaintances. There is no knowing what he might have done, and at any rate he wore a black Portuguese hat and had a negro servant. Some of the material for this castle he took from the Nijo palace which he had built for the Shogun Ashikaga Yoshiaki. For when he deposed him it stood empty and Nobunaga resumed about half of it, and this palace itself was constructed of materials appropriated from various temples in Kyoto. Japanese architecture is as adaptable as the people themselves and the withdrawal of comparatively few mortises will turn a temple into a mansion and vice versa. The tiles of the Azuchi keep were also said to have been gilt up to the fifth story, and fragments of tiles of this kind have been turned up on the site.

Hideyoshi's great castle of Osaka was built in 1584 on the site of Ishiyama, the fortified position held by the Hongwanji monks and which Nobunaga had no time to deal with after he took it. It was an even better place than Azuchi, with rivers on three sides and the river Yodo giving access to the sea. Inside this two more concentric moats

---

[5] The keep of Okayama castle, built about the same time, by Ukita, is said to be a replica of it.

were made. Nothing now remains of the castle, which had a five-storied keep and was about seven miles in circumference, for it was burnt and never rebuilt. There was the Hon-maru, Ni-no-maru, Yamasato-maru and San-no-maru, four wards in all. Hideyoshi requisitioned materials and labour from all the Daimyos of western Japan to construct it, and the size of some of the stones is remarkable. Several used in the gates measure 9 by 18 feet, and there is another 25 feet long, reaching from the base of the gate to the bottom of the lower story of the tower above. The gates of these castles were surrounded by massive stone walls like a box—hence the name for them, "Masugata" or "rice measure." Those entering were faced by a blank wall opposite, and the exit was through the side wall at right angles to it. Above these walls were works from which missiles could be shot from all sides into the enclosure as well as in front of it. Sometimes there was a barbican (*de-maru* or projecting ward), as at Osaka where it was called Sanada-maru after the designer Sanada Yukimura—one of the greatest experts in fortification of the day, who defended Osaka against Ieyasu and fell with it.

Other notable castles that belong to this age are Himeji, Okayama, Hiroshima and Hikone, the last being remarkable for its balcony and ornamental ogee windows in the upper story like the Kinkakuji, Kagoshima, Kumamoto, Wakamatsu, Nagoya, Matsuyama, Matsue, Fukuoka and some others. Edo castle also, the largest of all, was already being built and was of the same type. The building of this and many of the castles above mentioned almost simultaneously, in the early years of the seventeenth century, was one of the ways employed by Ieyasu to empty the pockets of the Daimyos and render them innocuous. For a castle was not built by the owner alone; his neighbours were all involved. These great castles were those of the lords of a whole province but there were lesser ones belonging to Daimyos who had only part of a province and who were therefore known as Castle Lords. Those who could not afford a castle had a fortified mansion and were known as Territorial Lords.

The styles in this period are all mixed and the details highly ornate so that in many cases this quality obscures the functional use of the elements. The tie-beams and beam-ends are richly carved often so that they lose their constructive shape. The beam-ends become more realistically elephant-headed and less suggestive than before, from the influence of the Kara style, and are often put where they are not needed merely as an extra decoration. The frog-crotches are carved in open-work as a rule, and are often weak looking in the legs and not very functional, for they do not look equal to supporting the weight above them. They often have a bracket capital on top that holds an elbow over it and this in turn supports the beam. The king-posts, too, are over-ornamented and sometimes introduced where unnecessary. The same may be said of the rafter brackets (*tabasami*). They are beauti-fully carved with flowers and angels in clouds and so on, but they seem to cling precariously to the rafters rather than hold them up.

CHAPTER X

EDO PERIOD (1616-1860)

THE early part of the Edo era does not differ much in its architecture from the Momoyama period, since those craftsmen and artisans who had worked for the Toyotomis continued to work for the Tokugawas. So things went on without much change till about 1700, when a great deterioration set in. The Tokugawa era was one of complete peace for some two hundred and fifty years, unbroken either by revolt within or assault from without. Few dynasties can have been so fortunate and few have had stronger or abler rulers in the early stages to found and consolidate their administration. For it is a great mistake to think that Ieyasu was the only strong and capable ruler of the line. Actually of the first five Shoguns who carried on the administration until after 1700, i.e. Ieyasu, Hidetada, Iemitsu, Ietsuna and Tsunayoshi, only the fourth, Ietsuna, was an easy-going character who did not care for ruling, with the result that an energetic and imperious minister, who was a relative, did it for him. The Shoguns had capable men about them and were well served in most things; and naturally the best of the hereditary architect-craftsmen entered their service. Of such a family was Heinai Masanobu who worked on the Nikko shrines in this capacity; his father Yoshimasa had worked on the Kōdaiji and the Toyokuni shrine where Hideyoshi was commemorated, and his grandfather Tameyoshi had built the Imperial Envoy Gate of the Jūraku mansion where he lived.

The work of this period was vigorous enough at first, but gradually everything became stereotyped and conventional, and there was no stimulus from abroad to revive it. After 1700 there was a mere repetition of detail that became weaker and more ornate in both temple and mansion, and only perhaps the Tea Masters preserved a tradition of simple elegance, though even they were by no means unaffected by the general laxity of things.

As time went on the Samurai or military class, who after 1600 or so became an hereditary caste and were forbidden to trade, became poorer and the trading class wealthier and more influential, in spite of the efforts of the government to prevent it by legislation. The result was that the soldier tended to lose his feeling for stern simplicity. Neither Nobunaga nor Hideyoshi had had time to regulate the lives of the people to the same extent as the Tokugawas, and this period is remarkable for its ever-increasing crop of detailed restrictions in the interest of economy and of the proper distinctions to be preserved between the different classes of people. Such economy and distinctions being, of course, for the benefit of the rulers. So from the great Daimyo to the small farmer their way of life came to be prescribed for them by the Gō Roju, the Great Council of the Shogun, and the houses they lived in, as well as the clothes they wore and the food they ate and the toys their children were to be allowed to play with, were carefully specified according to its views. It was all with the object of weakening any possible opposition to the dynasty and carrying out the policy of the supremacy of the Tokugawa house before everything, as laid down by the great founder Ieyasu. There had been so much civil war and general confusion for more than a century that these precautions were perhaps understandable on the principle of the proverb that "One who has been burnt will blow even on a salad." Crafts were hereditary and were strictly regulated and the apprentice had to copy exactly what his master taught him and not to depart from it on pain of expulsion. This repressed any originality though it cultivated technical skill. So the proportions of every part of a building became standardized and fixed and no great skill was required to reproduce them, which resulted in a general sameness everywhere. There was quite as much painting and carving as before, but there was a loss of freshness in these adjuncts; they were applied mechanically, so that the painting lost its decorative quality and the architecture its structural meaning.

At the same time some new types developed, such as theatres, colleges, inns and also public baths and restaurants. There was a great improvement in domestic architecture, for the people who had never been able before to live in anything but primitive dwellings with mud walls and board floors and no ceilings now became better off under the orderly government of the Tokugawas. As their standard of living rose they built themselves more comfortable and even luxurious houses —and this in spite of legislation to hinder them, for the power of money began to make itself felt even against the privileged position of the military aristocrats and officials, who were so often in debt to the rich merchants. So as the architectural ambit had in former days passed from the temple to the great mansion, now it widened out to include the dwellings of the ordinary people.

The Tokugawa Shoguns were Lords of the Empire as no military man had ever been before them. They held a centralized administration in their hands with an increasingly tenacious grip, and the land was enmeshed in a network of rules and checks that converted it into a vast barrack system, the control of which was all concentrated in Edo. Around the Shogun's castle the Daimyos had their residences—three at least for the great lords, Upper, Middle and Lower Yashikis, as they were called—where they lived when they were not at their castles in the provinces. For the regulation was that they should spend alternate years in each, except perhaps if they were ill, when they might be excused if the Shogun's doctors who examined them reported their indisposition to be sufficiently serious.

Encouraged as they were by the government to spend money on buildings, except fortified ones (for none might rebuild or repair his castle without permission, which was not likely to be given), their mansions and gardens were extensive and splendid. The Shogun also frequently honoured them by allowing them to build or contribute to the building or restoration of some great shrine or temple, or it might be the Imperial Palace; so ever more of their income went into construction, especially as Japan is a land where fires are almost epidemic, and proverbially so in Edo. They were consequently often hard put to it for funds, "being at his shifts for money to go up to Edo," as the chief of the English factory at Hirado said of the lord of this place about the second decade of the seventeenth century.

But the country had peace and no funds were needed for war, and soon the various castle towns, which largely date from this time, became miniature replicas of Edo, even to the names of their streets. Actually Edo itself was only a very big castle town, for Ieyasu made the same kind of capital for the country as he had had for his province, and installed the same type of government there, administering the Empire out of his own pocket just as a feudal lord did with his fief.

Ieyasu had taken in hand the small castle he found in Edo when he entered it in 1590 and later resolved to make his capital there, far removed from the enervating Court atmosphere of Kyoto. With the assistance of Honda, his secretary, and Tōdō, his old friend, he reconstructed it and the town so that it was and is one of the greatest fortified areas in the world. Most of the work on it was done between 1600 and 1614, and included cutting away the top of Kanda Hill and throwing it into the sea to fill in the low-lying ground by Hibiya and make up what is now the lower or business part of the city. The higher and better part was occupied by the castle and the residences of the many Daimyos and the Shogun's own household troops and their officers (Hatamoto). Owing to its uneven site it was not possible to lay out Edo in the same regular chess-board fashion as Kyoto, though where possible the streets were made on this principle. As in other cities the various trades tended to be found together in the same streets which were called after them, Timber Yard Street, Sword Polishers' Street, Tub-makers' Street and so on. There was a quarter where the theatres were to be found, and another where the temples of the various sects lined up expectantly to receive contributions. There was also the pleasure quarter of the restaurants and brothels which was an enclosure with only one entrance, strictly guarded and patrolled by the government constabulary and spies, because there the criminal and the revolutionary were most likely to be found and caught. When Ieyasu died in 1616 the city was much what it continued to be except for the outer moat which the third Shogun Iemitsu added—at the expense of the Daimyos, of course. It is calculated that the cost of the city to them was somewhere about the equivalent of £100,000,000.

Edo castle, the seat of the Shogun and the centre of the autocratic centralized government of Japan for more than two hundred and fifty years, was of the same type as the other great castles, and had the same wide moats and massive walls and gates as Osaka. But in size few fortified cities in the world compare with it, except Peking, Constantinople, and perhaps Daulatabad.[1] There was the Hon-maru with its keep and the subsidiary wards, the Ni-no-maru and San-no-maru, in one block where the Shogun and his large family and household lived, and where the councillors and high officials came to carry on the affairs

---

[1] It measured roughly 6000 yards east to west and 4100 yards north to south Its circumference was about 10 miles

of State and the great lords repaired to pay their respects. Adjoining it, but separated by another moat and wall system, was the Nishi-maru or Western Castle where the heir to the Shogun or the Retired Shogun lived, and which also contained a large space given up to the secondary mausolea of the late Shoguns; behind this was the Fukiage park or pleasance where the inmates of the castle could enjoy all the advantages of the secluded country while living in the centre of a city of a million or so inhabitants. This Nishi-maru is now the Imperial Palace.

Ieyasu, who loved simplicity and economy as, according to him, Heaven also did, was content to live in a modest style compared with that of his successors, though naturally the dignity of his office required a certain amount of ceremony and display. Hidetada, his son, did not depart much from his ways. It was in the days of Iemitsu the son of Hidetada that the architectural splendour of the period began to shine in Edo and Nikko. None of the original buildings inside Edo castle have survived, though the moats and walls and many of the towers and gates have remained unchanged and lend an air of great dignity to the Imperial Precincts. But in Kyoto the Nijō castle still preserves the great reception rooms and decoration of the time of Ieyasu, for it was erected then as an outpost of the Shogun in the old capital, from which his officials could dominate it and where he could go and stay when he himself visited the city.

The Shogun's palace was divided into three sections, the O-omote or Great Outer Palace which contained the chief reception chambers for public audience and the apartments of some officials and guards; the Naka-oku or Middle Interior which contained audience chambers for more intimate receptions of Shogunal relatives or great lords, and also the apartments where the councillors sat and met, and where the Shogun transacted the business of government; and lastly the O-oku or Great Interior tenanted only by ladies, where the Shogun retired to relax after the strenuous work of administration. Here were the apartments for the Shogun's wife and mother and his ladies-in-waiting and for all the lesser lady officials who waited on these and the maids who waited on them. It was separated from the Naka-oku by a bronze partition and specially guarded gates. None of the male officials were allowed to enter here, and communication between the inner and outer palaces was maintained by small boys. The plan of the outer palace here given has no exact date,[2] and there are two versions of it that differ in some details but have substantially the same arrangement of rooms. Since one of these has notes ascribing some of the interior decoration to Kano Tannyu (1602-1674), it may be that of the castle as it was before it was destroyed by the great fire of 1657, or of the new building put up again in 1659 in the space of six months or so.

As to the O-oku, there are two plans also that differ considerably in their arrangement. One given in the *Edo Jidai Shiron* or *Essays on the Edo Period*, issued by the Japanese Historical and Geographical Association and stated to be of the Genroku era (1688-1704), and another a copy of one by Kora Buzen, chief carpenter of the construction department of the Shogun, an office that was hereditary in the Kora family. In the second plan there is a far more regular and barrack-like layout of the suits and apartments of the ladies-in-waiting and their attendants, which are placed in long rows one behind the other called *naga-tsubone* or barrack suites. It might perhaps be the O-oku of somewhere about the year 1800.

The front or outer part of the O-oku was taken up by five separate sets of apartments which were the living and ceremonial audience chambers of the Shogun and his wife, children and close relatives. The suites (*b*) and (*c*) were the most formal audience chambers, and (*a*) was the suite where they usually lived. The (*d*) suite is the guest suite, presumably used to receive lady connexions of the highest rank, and (*e*) consists of living-rooms. Since most of these were used by the Shogun or his wife they had dais and lower dais chambers though they were only for ceremony, and the sitting-rooms behind were actually used as living-rooms. Each suite had its dressing-rooms and bath-rooms, store-rooms and ante-chambers. The ante-chamber was where the attendants sat while serving meals or conversing with those on the higher level, and the third chamber was where they retired to sit when not needed. Each of these suites with its corridors and *irikawa* (matted corridor) occupied not less than 200 mats. Next to them lay the kitchen quarters, also furnished with sitting-rooms and ante-rooms with upper and lower chambers like the rest, since on occasions they would be visited by the Shogun's wife, whose official title was

---

[2] Plan in Mitsuhashi's *Riso no Kaoku,* vol. i.

Mi-daidōkoro or the August Lady of the Kitchen.[3] Beyond this again was another suite (*f*) with reception and sitting-rooms and kitchen complete. The Shogun's bathroom is described as being 12 feet by 15 feet, with a dressing-room of six mats adjoining. It was of pure white *hinoki* wood, with two tubs of white wood having green bamboo hoops on black lacquer stands for hot and cold water respectively. The decorations of all the audience chambers and other rooms were in the ornate Shōin style of lacquered wood and coffered and double coffered ceilings and gilt and painted *fusuma,* as can be seen in the Nijo palace which is the sole survivor of this type, though specimens may be seen in the ceremonial reception rooms of great temples.

Behind these suites the whole of the remaining space in the O-oku was taken up by the *tsubone* or lodgings of the ladies of various ranks who were the sole tenants of this extensive area. The larger suites for the more important lady officials seem to be situated nearest the Shogunal apartments and the smaller ones farther away. The largest have three apartments with a boarded space with kitchen, scullery, etc., and behind this the back rooms for the maids. These suites were evidently occupied by more than one lady in many cases, for it is stated that ladies attached to the Shogun had no private rooms but boarded with the seniors. The number of these senior lady officials is given as seventy-seven at the beginning of the eighteenth century. These were the officials who had the privilege of audience with the Shogun and his wife, and did not include the personal ladies-in-waiting of the latter. The total number of inhabitants of the O-oku was probably more than a thousand.

In the outer palace the Great Audience Chamber,[4] the Shiro Shōin or White Suite and the Kuro Shōin or Black Suite lay one behind the

---

[3] With the same significance as the Kita-no-mandōkoro of the Kamakura period.

[4] There is a description of its use when the fifth Shogun Tsunayoshi held an investigation there in 1681: "The Shogun took his seat on the middle dais of the Great Hall of Audience while on the lower dais sat the heads of the Three Houses (of the Tokugawa Family) with the chancellor in attendance on them. In the ante-chamber were the vassal lords with captains of the guards and commanders of the household troops. In the western veranda were the junior councillors, the Confucian professors, the chamberlains, secretaries and officials of the Middle Interior. On the eastern veranda were the lords-in-waiting of the Black Reception Chamber, the censors and envoys. Lastly on the lower veranda sat a councillor with the shrine and temple commissioners, the chief censor and his staff."

other on the left side, and behind these again the Goza-no-ma or Sitting Room Suite and the Kyusoku-no-ma or Retiring Room Suite for less formal occasions. Outside lords who were not related to the Shogun were received in the Pine Chamber, or Willow Chamber, the Tairo or chancellor in the Tamari, the Three Shogunal Branch Houses in the White Shōin, while the new year reception for the household was held in the Black Suite, and so on.

In size Edo castle stood about midway between the palace of Peking and the Seraglio of Istambul, but unlike both of these it harboured no eunuchs[5] and certainly no foreigners.

But the best known works of the Edo period are undoubtedly the shrines of Nikko. Tokugawa Ieyasu, the founder of all this peace and prosperity, had been deified after his death in 1616 as Tōshōgu Dai-Gongen, or Great Manifestation of Buddha Resplendent in the Eastern Region, and as Ancestral Deity of the actually ruling house, he was the best served deity in the country. Therefore he had to have a suitable shrine, and this was provided by his grandson Iemitsu who had the greatest reverence for his divine grandfather. Ieyasu had been buried at Kunōzan, a hill overlooking the sea near Shizouka where he died, but was transferred a year afterwards to Nikko in Shimozuke, as he had arranged before he died, or perhaps as the monk Tenkai, his spiritual adviser, had arranged after. The shrine at Kunōzan is like a miniature edition of Nikko, but is comparatively little known.

And in this way a new architectural style was created, that of the mausoleum shrine called after Ieyasu "Gongen style" and composed of a mixture of Buddhist temple, Shinto shrine and stupa tomb. Every known type of spiritual housing was piled up to do honour to this great soldier-statesman. The shrine itself is, as before stated, modelled on the Kaisando of the Eihōji temple, or the shrines that were influenced by it like Kitano, and to this were added spacious courts like a temple, with splendid gates, bell-tower and drum-tower, pagoda, treasure house, library, stable and every other sacred appurtenance that could be thought of. Then behind the main shrine, which consists of oratory, stone chamber, and sanctuary (Haiden, Ishi-no-ma and Honden), and approached by long flights of stone steps, is the actual tomb, a bronze

---

[5] Their place was taken by capable and strong-minded old lady officials who were at least as efficient and certainly more honest. They were the successors of the lady Kasuga who organized the inner palace under Ieyasu, whose confidante she was and of whom she was in some sort the female counterpart.

stupa pagoda of the Yugi type, with a bronze altar on which stand the usual candlestick, censer and flower vase, the whole enclosed in a smaller court with gates of solid bronze. There is no decoration here, not a glint. The atmosphere is one of hardness and endurance, the prominent qualities of the "Divine Lord." It is a curious contrast with the casket of Hidetada, his son, whose mausoleum is at Shiba in Tokyo; for Hidetada's stupa is the same shape, but inside a shrine and very much larger, while it is covered everywhere with designs in raised gold lacquer. It is about 20 feet high and is said to be the largest piece of gold lacquer in the world. A similar shrine was built for Iemitsu beside it, and for the rest of the Shoguns, thirteen in all, there were a series of others at Shiba and Ueno in Edo at the temples of Zōzōji and Kaneiji respectively. There was another series, too, though much smaller, at Momiji-yama within the Western castle. And these latter were copied, like most other things, by the great Daimyos who had their own mausolea in their provinces, of the same type, but on a much more modest scale. Their actual tombs were not of the stupa pagoda order, but stone monuments representing the Five Elements.

It may be noted here that Imperial Mausolea have almost no architectural features, for the Sovereigns were buried in natural hills in the manner of the ancient tumulus, and this has only a fence, *torii* and gate. The Kōdaiji temple, where the departed spirit of Hideyoshi was revered, was in some sense a mausoleum, but more in the style of the temples built for somewhat the same purpose by the Fujiwaras, as places where services might be performed that the departed great one might obtain enlightenment. But the Nikko shrines were the beginning of a new, or rather revised and adapted, cult of the deified military dictator on the lines of the deified Sovereign; for it was not long before the Shoguns petitioned for and obtained from the Imperial Court the dispatch of an Imperial Envoy every year to Nikko, thus putting it on a level with the Ise shrine of the Sun Goddess, the only other shrine to which such an honour was paid. Hidetada had built the first shrine at Nikko in 1617, but this was quite small, and the present structures were begun by Iemitsu in 1623. It took thirteen years to finish the work. The name of the chief carpenter was Kora Bungo-no-kami Munehiro, head of the Shogun's office of works, an office that became hereditary in his family. There were also two Daimyos appointed as

Lord High Commissioners to be in general charge of affairs and to have authority to order anything that was needed. The buildings comprise the outer court with the Nio Gate, the middle court with the Yōmei Gate and the inner court with the Kara Gate. The Sakashita Gate leads from the second court to the tomb. In the inner court are the shrine buildings and in the others are the Kagura Stage where the sacred dance is performed before the Deity, the Goma or Fire Offering Hall, the Deity's Palanquin House, the Honchi Hall, the bell- and drum-towers, the library, three storehouses, the ablution tank, the stable for the Deity's horse, and the five-storied pagoda.

The main shrine is 30 feet square, of which 12 square feet comprise the outer sanctuary (Gaijin) and the remaining 18 square feet the inner sanctuary (Naijin), within which is the Holy of Holies (Nai-Naijin). In these the work is of the finest imaginable, but they are not now accessible to any one but the ritualists and members of the family. The decoration is all of raised gold lacquer and the pillars are ornamented with overlaid work with dragon, pine and bamboo motifs, enriched with carving and silver gilt mountings wherever possible. The connecting stone chamber, floored with granite, is 18 feet square. The Haiden or oratory is 54 by 24 feet with a space of 30 feet in the centre for the main oratory, and separate ones for the Shogun and Imperial Abbot on each side of it, 12 feet wide respectively. The ceilings and other decorations of these, which are on view, are also exceedingly fine, the two side chambers being panelled with carvings of rare wood. All the pillars of these chambers and the rest of the buildings are lacquered in black and the woodwork is plastered and lacquered in gold and colours outside as well as in. Even the floors are in black or red lacquer. The ceilings are coved and double coved and coffered with designs of birds and beasts done in gold lacquer and colours in the coffers, and everywhere there are the usual ornamental metal mounts.

The Yōmei-mon or Sun-bright Gate has often been described and more often illustrated. It is the most elaborate of all the portals. It is a two-storied gate, hipped and gabled on each of its four sides, and as complicated as such a roof can be. The construction is almost hidden by the carving in openwork, high and low relief, and in the round, that reminds one almost of a Hindu temple for profuseness, lacquered and coloured from the eaves downwards. It is covered with ornamental work of every description applied wherever a place can be found for it. In all Japan there is no such riot of coloured carvings. Man and all the flora and fauna are represented in it. Professor Amanuma observes, "There is plenty to investigate in it," but he does not, I think, admire it.

All the other buildings are in the same style. Of all perhaps the canopy of the ablution tank is the most impressive, because the decoration does not detract from the construction and the line and proportion are fine. It is worthy of the plain stone tank it covers, over which the water flows evenly like a veil of crystal over all four sides. The five-storied pagoda is lacquered and painted red from top to toe, like everything else at Nikko. It was presented by Sakai Tadakatsu, a loyal councillor and relative of the Tokugawa house, and is 113 feet 3-1/5 inches high with a *sōrin* of 25 feet. This is only about 1/5 of the total, whereas in the ancient pagodas it was about half—for example, in that of the Daigōji. Its proportions therefore are not so satisfying; but in its internal construction the arrangement of the beams and ties to ensure stability and absorb the shocks of wind and earthquake is advanced to near perfection.

Everywhere the Nikko shrines are a triumph of technical craftsmanship of the same type as was employed by Hideyoshi in the Momoyama age, but of a far more profuse and gorgeous kind. Certainly they do not compare with the splendid proportions and simple dignity of the earlier unadorned constructional work. But in a sense they are practical and efficient enough, and set in the background of dark green cryptomeria covered hills they appear less gaudy than they would on a plain. And the colours are rich and· well blended. It evidently needs people who prefer black and white to manage colour properly. And it must not be forgotten that their purpose was to glorify the deified founder of the Tokugawa line, certainly one of the greatest figures who ever ruled in Japan or anywhere else, who had practically become the most important Deity in the land. As propaganda for him they are successful enough, for now they attract visitors from every part of the world, as does also Taira Kiyomori's favourite shrine of Miyajima. But that is not all. With all their fine lacquer and carvings exposed to the weather they needed constant repair, and work on them has practically never ceased since the time they were built. All this had to be paid for by the Daimyos, who were granted the honour of being allowed to do it, and whose purses became more and more anaemic in consequence. Only that aspect of them may be said to represent the spirit of the economical Ieyasu, for otherwise they are according to the taste of the gorgeous and luxurious Iemitsu, the first unapproachable autocrat of the line.[6]

His own shrine, known as the Taiyuin from his posthumous title, was begun in 1652 and was finished in about three years. Sakai Tadakatsu was the High Commissioner and Heinai Masanobu the architect. It is in just the same style as the Tōshogu, but with a difference in detail. For instance the Honden interior is like the Buddha Hall of a Zen temple with a dragon painted on the ceiling and a two-storied Buddhist shrine on the altar. Also the connecting chamber is an *ai-no-ma* (stone-floored chamber) on the same level as the Haiden. In several other points, too, it reveals Zen influence. It is therefore not exactly true Gongen style, but modified. But Iemitsu was an aesthete who was very fond of Chanoyu which has strong Zen affinities.

Beside the Nikko shrines other buildings well known to the Western world are the Great Buddha Hall of the Tōdaiji at Nara, the largest wooden building in the world, 250 feet square over the eaves and 170 feet high; the main temple of the Chionin at Kyoto and its fine Sammon; the temple of Kiyomizu, also at Kyoto; the main temple and pagoda of Asakusa in Tokyo; and the pagoda at Ueno, the only relic of Kaneiji. There are also the Kondo of the West Hongwanji at Kyoto and the gate of the Nanzenji in the same city. Of these the Tōdaiji Buddha Hall is in the Tenjiku style, a copy from Kamakura, but otherwise this style like the Kara has died out, a thoroughly mixed one only remaining; but the Wa style was known as the Shi-tennoji, and the Kara as the Kenninji after these temples.

A peculiar type of which there are few examples is that of the Mampukuji, begun by the Chinese priest Ingen in 1661, directly imported from the Ming dynasty of his country. It is of the Obaku sect of Zen and is on an extremely regular plan. There are three more of these Obaku temples in Nagasaki, of which the Sūfukuji is the finest.

---

[6] This aspect of the Nikko architecture was apparently unknown to or overlooked by Tout when he was puzzled that the same period could produce these shrines and the Katsura Imperial Villa, the high watermark of simple good taste. The functions of the two are quite different. One was a Daimyo-impoverishing advertisement for the Shogun and the other a quiet retreat for the Emperor.

Their Chinese character is much more marked than is that of the Mampukuji and it is said that the great gate of the Sūfukuji was made in China and sent to Japan in pieces for erection. Most of the temples of the Tokugawa period, however, have no particular layout but are adapted to their sites. The Myōshinji at Kyoto is a fine example of a Zen temple most of which belongs to this era, though there is one part of late Momoyama origin. It is a good specimen of the regular plan of the temples of this sect and has a fine refectory and kitchen.

The Imperial Palace went on being destroyed by fire as before and then rebuilt in much the same way, but after the great Kyoto fire of 1781 the eleventh Shogun Ienari, who greatly reverenced the Imperial House, gave orders for it to be rebuilt on a very much more magnificent scale in the style of the Heian period. It was begun in 1789 and took about three years to finish. The work was under the superintendence of the great statesman Matsudaira Sadanobu, the Shogun's Premier, who took great pains in making research to discover just how the ancient palace had been arranged. But in 1854 it was burnt again and then rebuilt about three years after in the same way, and this is the present palace. Since the Emperor has now gone to live in what was the castle of the Shogun in Edo, renamed Tokyo, it is not used and can be inspected; but the Accession Ceremony must be held there, since the Imperial Castle (Kyūjō) at Tokyo does not contain a Shishinden, where alone this ceremony can be performed.

The Shūgaku Detached Palace, which can also be seen, is a spring and autumn villa presented by the Shogun Hidetada to the Emperor Go Mizu-no-ō (who designed its garden) as a country resort, and still remains in its original state.

Another type of building introduced by Tokugawa Tsunayoshi, the fifth Shogun (1681), was the Seido or College of Confucius. Confucianism was the official philosophy of the Tokugawas, and the fifth Shogun was particularly enthusiastic about it, giving regular lectures every month to the Daimyos, who thus had another tribulation inflicted on them. The Seido was a simple building in rather Chinese style and had a Hall of Confucius with a bronze statue of the sage. The example of the Shogun was naturally imitated by the Daimyos, and Confucian colleges after the same pattern sprang up in the various fiefs, where the children of the Samurai retainers were taught the Chinese classics.

They were a sort of Japanese public school. That built by Ikeda Mitsu-masa at Okayama was the first.

To prevent if possible the destruction of valuables by fire, the Kura or fireproof storehouse attached to temples, residences and particularly tradesmen's shops was evolved. It is usually of two stories with very thick walls of mud covered outside with the same hard white plaster, or diagonal black tiling with white plaster joints, that was so much used for the outer walls of noblemen's mansions and those of the greater Samurai.[7] The Kura has small windows with iron shutters and a heavy door like a safe. In some cases the tiled roof is detachable. It may be connected with the house by a covered way, and in it all the pictures, pottery, lacquer ware, tea utensils, books, curios and, in the case of the Samurai, swords and armour, were kept. It has had therefore a certain influence on the Japanese habit of continually changing their pictures and utensils instead of keeping them all about them in their rooms as Europeans do. It is consequently a simple matter to alter the atmosphere of a room completely by this device, especially if, as is the case in large houses, the *fusuma* are changed as well.

Edo houses were orginally roofed with wooden shingles and thatch like farm-houses, for the city developed very rapidly when, from a small town, it was suddenly promoted to be the capital of the Empire. All the great lords had to build mansions and live there practically as hostages with many of their retainers, and it was not easy to house this sudden influx of people of all sorts very substantially. But the constant fires led the Shogun to issue an order that all dwellings should be tiled. It was the fourth Shogun Ietsuna (1660) who found Edo shingled and left it tiled.

The public bath house[8] was another institution that became popular from this time and has always remained one of the characteristic features of Japan. Hot baths and hot springs date from the Heian period or before, it seems, but the bath house business developed in the big cities. Here it in some sort performs the functions of the public house, for it is a place where all are accustomed to meet on terms of

---

[7] Known as *namako-kabe* or bêche-de-mer wall from the resemblance of the convex joints to this creature. Cf., *namako-kawara,* a cover tile.

[8] It was commonly called Yuya (Hot Water Shop) or Furoya (Bath Shop). It had for a sign a bow and arrow, because *iru* means "to shoot" as well as "to enter."

nudist equality and enliven the time with chat and humour. Its name in Edo was Sento or "one cent hot water," so it was an amusement that could be indulged in by every one. The great, naturally, did not attend it, for they had bathrooms attached to their own residences; but the middle classes, though they often had this convenience too, went to the Yuya for the entertainment they obtained there. These bath houses consist of a large room with a place at the entrance for depositing clothes, and a high seat for the custodian on top of the partition which separates the men's side from that of the women, so that he is in a commanding position to overlook everything and take the money. A curtain may divide this part from the other portion of the room, or it may not. At the other end is the square wooden tank, usually covered in by a gabled canopy such as is seen in Hideyoshi's bathroom and called a Zakuro-guchi or Pomegranate Mouth, possibly because it spread wide and revealed everything, as that fruit is proverbially said to do.

Before long these bath houses had rooms above, where liquor and light refreshment were served by not unattractive waitresses, thus approximating more closely to a tavern or restaurant. But the government did not approve of this and prohibited them on the pretext that they would be a cause of dissipation to the Samurai; the real reason was that they were outside the pleasure quarter where amusement was government-controlled and spied upon.

The streets of Edo were furnished with gates at the cross-roads each with a guard-house (Tsuji-ban or Cross-road Guard) so that they could all be shut off should any disturbance take place, or the authorities wish to arrest any one, or the Shogun proceed through the main street which was then cleared. These gates are the prototype, presumably of the modern police-box system. There was a very efficient force of Samurai constabulary and detectives in Edo who worked under the supervision of the two City Commissioners.

The immediate neighbourhood of the castle and many other parts of the city as well were largely taken up by the mansions of the greater and lesser Daimyos with their imposing gates on the street front. And since everything in this society was regulated the Daimyos' gates had to be built according to their standing and income, and by their shape indicated what sort of a lord lived there. It will be noted that the highest rank was shown by a pair of hipped gables on the roofs of the guard-houses that projected at each side of the entrance, and that an ordinary gable indicated a lesser rank. Lower down still the guard-house lost its foundation and became an oriel window, while those of smaller incomes were allowed only one of these. All these fronts and gates were of plain wood after the early days, when they had apparently been often gilt and lacquered—the exception being a very great lord related by marriage with the Shogun who was allowed to paint his gate red.[9] All below the rank of Daimyo (i.e. lower than 10,000 *koku*) had to have a plain front to their gate-house without any of these projections. If a feudal mansion was destroyed by fire it was not allowed to be rebuilt as before, but in a simpler way with an unroofed gate as a penalty for carelessness. Beside the castle towers and a few pagodas the only noticeable feature of the Edo skyline was the fire-tower in each district which contained a bell that was rung with an increasing number of strokes to the minute in ratio of nearness to the fire.

Along the street front of the feudal mansions ran the "long-house" barracks (*nagaya*) in which the retainers lived round their lord. They were often diagonally tiled about half way up the outside wall and were either of white plaster or black weatherboard with wooden ribs laid vertically over it above.

Of the three or more mansions a Daimyo maintained, the one in Daimyo Street (Daimyo Kōji) outside the castle gates, or near one of the other gates, was the Upper Mansion where he would stay while he had business at the castle paying calls or otherwise being in attendance, or if he held office as councillor and so on. The Middle Mansion was usually a little farther away, and so had more room for gardens and also housed the vassals of lesser importance and the family. The Lower Mansion was in the suburbs and had not as a rule such large buildings or place for many retainers, but was set in an extensive garden and used as a place of diversion away from the crowded city. The residence of the lord himself lay back across the courtyard behind the front gate, and was entered by the usual porch with pillars supporting the projecting roof of Chinese gable form over the *shikidai* or boarded platform in front of the entrance hall on which the servants

---

[9] This red gate still stands as the portal of the Imperial University of Tokyo, the site of which was formerly the mansion of this lord Maeda of Kaga, which at the restoration he presented to the government.

knelt to receive guests, as they still do. Inside there were the same Shōin reception rooms with *irikawa* and outer veranda and dais as in the Shogun's castle, but on a much smaller scale, and varying with the means and taste of the owner.

None of these mansions has survived in Tokyo, except the Hama Mansion by the Sea; but in some of the castle towns in the country there are Daimyo mansions or villas[10] like those at Hikone, now an inn, and Okayama and Hiroshima, now public parks. The residences of the Hatamoto or Shogun's high officers were of the same type also, but smaller and simpler again, and smallest and simplest of all were those of the ordinary Samurai which, however, were still built on the same plan. In the castle towns, as in Edo, the Samurai lived in certain quarters by themselves, and apart from those of the tradesmen, artisans, temples, theatres and amusement caterers. The smallest Samurai called *Ashigaru* or foot-soldiers lived in a set of streets called Bancho or "guard quarter" like that outside the castle at Edo. Those of higher rank lived nearer to the castle, and the streets they occupied were much wider than those used for trade or amusement—a narrow street for shopping and a broad one for military pomp and strategy, a most practical arrangement. In the hot summer days the narrow streets can be covered in by drawing canvas blinds across from one side to the other, and they also lend themselves to decoration with lanterns and other devices both by night and day in a way that leaves little to be desired.

Neither the Japanese shop nor the inn has departed as much from the plan of the private house as in Europe. The shop, called *mise* (show-place) or *tana* (shelf), is merely the house front opened to the street by raising the shutters and disclosing a matted space, with an earth floor below it in the same style as a kitchen. The customers stand on the earth floor or sit on the edge of the matted part, on which squat the shopkeeper and his assistants and on which are set out samples of his goods. Behind this is the house in which the master and some of the assistants live. It is very often separated from the shop by a court-yard garden. Shops vary a good deal according to the goods they sell, but this is the general plan.

Inns, too, are only like a large private house with many rooms,

---

[10] For views of these, see Harada's *The Lesson of Japanese Architecture*, pp. 43, 62, 99-105.

and sometimes a shop front added where the guests are received and the host often sits. But the best type of inn has not even this, but only a spacious porch like a mansion. There are no public rooms, for every one feeds and sleeps in his own room as at home. The only exception is the bathroom, and that is rather more public than the bath house since there is no division for men and women. Inns very often have fine interior decorations and also beautiful gardens such as are, I think, not so often found in Europe. The same thing applies to restaurants which, when in Japanese style, hardly differ much from inns, except that they do have rooms large enough to entertain a large party of people if necessary, though smaller groups prefer to have their meals privately in separate rooms. Public drinking shops hardly exist except in the sense that roadside tea-houses that sell tea and cakes and rice to travellers also sell liquor. In fact I think any one can sell liquor and tobacco if they wish at any hour, as on the continent of Europe, and their drinking habits are similar, so that there is nothing that one could describe as public-house architecture. The cities are not therefore disfigured, as are ours here, by the occupation of many of the best sites of the main thoroughfares by gin palaces, repellent as a rule to both eye and nose, and sometimes an embarrassment to law and order. The roadside tea-house in Japan, though it is not exactly architecture, is as well mannered as more permanent structures and rather adorns than defaces the countryside. This is apparent from the many charming illustrations in which it figures in the black-and-white illustrated guide-books to Edo, the Tokaido road, etc., called *Meisho Zue* or *Pictures of Famous Places* and published about 1800.

CHAPTER XI

THE SHOGUN'S RECEPTION OF THE EMPEROP

ON the twenty-first day of the ninth month of the year 1438 the Emperor Go Hanazono deigned to visit the Shogun Yoshinori, who prepared four rooms on the eastern side of the Shinden for the Imperial use. Wide matting was spread on the floors and there were screens and curtains and the *mi-chodai* (a four-post canopy over the seat or bed of the master) was put there for His Majesty's sleeping chamber. The rest of the Shinden was for the Emperor's living-room suite (Tsune no Goza-sho). On the twenty-second day there was a performance of Bugaku[1] in the western court, after which His Majesty repaired to the *tai* or adjoining building and a banquet was served. Following that there was a poem-composing party that continued till late at night.

On the twenty-third there was another performance of Bugaku in the courtyard. The former performance had been given by courtiers of both the higher and also the lower ranks (those who had not the right of entering the Imperial Presence); but to-day only these latter took part and both the courtiers of the Imperial Suite and the Shogun and his household were graciously permitted to view it.

On the twenty-fourth it rained and nothing particular was done, only they feasted all day in the six rooms of the Shinden. On the twenty-fifth His Majesty viewed a game of football from the western veranda and then there was a banquet within the screen, after which there were parties for Japanese poems, Chinese poems and music, given on three boats. His Majesty proceeded from the eastern door of the southern veranda to the boat on matting that was laid down by the officers of the Kamon department. The courtiers preceded him carrying lanterns and the Chujo[2] bore the Imperial Sword. The Kambaku,[3] the former Kambaku Kaneyoshi and the Shogun and his suite were in attendance. The Emperor proceeded to the boat for Japanese poems.

---

[1] An operatic performance.   [2] Court title.   [3] Chancellor.

On it was a high pavilion with two phoenixes, and two pieces of white jade on pedestals decorated the prow. The boat for Chinese poems had a dragon figure-head and that for music had a water-fowl. And there was the man in the moon with a Chinese crown. Round the lake and on the island were cressets that lit up the scene, along the western eaves of the mansion were hung lanterns that threw reflections on to the water, and the ladies-in-waiting on His Majesty with those in attendance on the Shogun and his consort came out on the south-west veranda to see it. When the music was over they proceeded to a part at the end of the Reception Room (Go Kaisho) where a temporary Izumi Dono had been made and were entertained by recitations of Chinese poetry.

On the twenty-fourth, the day of the Imperial Return, there was a banquet in the Go Kaisho and afterwards the Shogun presented His Majesty with a writing by Ono-no-Tōfu in a golden box suspended from a golden bough by a chain of jade. Beside this both the Shogun and his consort made large presents of gold and silver and costumes, and the courtiers of the Imperial Suite and the ladies-in-waiting all received very valuable gifts.

CHAPTER XII

BUILDING REGULATIONS IN THE TOKUGAWA PERIOD

AMONG the regulations of the various details of life in the Tokugawa period those about the limitation of the size and decoration of houses according to the rank and income of the individual bulk fairly large. It is probable, too, that there was more of it than appears in the published laws of the Shogunate, for much was done by local officials who had considerable power. The feudal lords issued these prohibitions when they were hard up, just as the Shogun did. In the very early days of the Shogunate there was no special legislation of this kind for the military class, and it is not until the time of the third Shogun Iemitsu that we meet with it. The farmers were no doubt too poor to need it before this, for it was the policy of the first Shogun so to tax them that they had no surplus at all—a condition, in his opinion, most conducive to hard work.

But in 1643 we find: "Those under 10,000 *koku*, even Bangashira (chief officers in a clan), must not have reception rooms more than 15 feet deep (2½ *ken*). But the kitchen may be 18 feet deep (3 *ken*). When houses are rebuilt it must be done according to this measurement" And it was not likely that any one else would have a larger one except a Daimyo whose income must be at least 10,000 *koku*. The average size of the farmer's house in early Tokugawa days was about 15 feet—that is, supposing the *ken* in which these measurements are given was 6 feet as later. But this is not quite certain, for the *ken* was 10 feet in the Kamakura age and later on was 9 and 7 feet.

Again in 1657 we find regulations for the dwellings of the people: "In building it is unnecessary to say that 'long houses' are not allowed, and living-rooms behind shops must not be more than 3 *ken* deep."

Then in 1668 there was an order about the building of temples:

(*a*) Three *ken* of Kyoto measure is the limit of depth, but the frontage may be as desired.

(*b*) The wing with the Buddhist shrine must not be more than three *ken* square, Kyoto measure.

(*c*) The lean-to veranda all round shall not be more than one and a half *ken*.

(*d*) The roof-ridge shall be a short one.

(*e*) There must be no construction above the bracketing.

No halls, guest-chambers, monks' residences or refectory kitchens shall be longer than the dimensions given. If it is desired to make them so the matter must be referred to the Shrine and Temple Commissioner for his decision.

Regulations for residences: The following are prohibited:

(*a*) Frieze beams.

(*b*) Cedar doors.

(*c*) Built-in Shōin windows.

(*d*) Fine and rare wood.

(*e*) Carving, openwork, carved bracketing or any elaborate ornament.

(*f*) Lacquering of the edges of the *tokonoma* or the use of Chinese paper for the sliding doors.

(*g*) Gates made of *keyaki* wood (*Zelkova acuminata*).

As to the temples, it appears that village temples or small ones are meant; but the rules about residences show that people were becoming comparatively well-to-do and apt to afford things that are the sign of superior rank.

In 1699 there is another order:

Those with incomes of from 3000 *koku* to 1000 *koku* are not to build houses exceeding 2½ *ken* in depth. And in future no carving, bracketing, or lacquering of the rims or beams of the *tokonoma* is allowed.

Walls set with stones are not allowed. But a *no-tsura* (rough stone wall) may be permitted where necessary.

For those below 1000 *koku* income 2 *ken* deep is the limit for rooms, and in future frieze beams, cedar doors, built-in Shōin windows, carving, bracketing and lacquering of the *tokonoma* edges and beams, and the use of Chinese paper for the *fusuma* is prohibited.

Again in 1716 the eighth Shogun Yoshimune, who had to enforce economy where possible, because the extravagance of his predecessors and the natural limitations of the Shogunate income had brought the country into financial difficulties, issued a set of regulations limiting the size of the house to 3 *ken* deep and forbidding the use of frieze beams and detached rooms, since luxury did not conduce to good farming. This also shows how the standard of living was rising, a fact that is rather confirmed by the observation of a *shoya* or large farmer in 1730. He says: "Thirty years or so ago most peasants lived in houses with earth floors and matting laid over it. But now we see not only boarded floors as well as ceilings, *tatami*, and waist-high *shōji*, but *shikidai*, outside verandas and landscape gardens as well."

CHAPTER XIII

SHŌJI, FUSUMA AND CEILINGS

SHŌJI AND FUSUMA

THE two words *shōji* and *fusuma* now mean the outside sliding doors covered with translucent paper (*akari-shōji* or light *shōji*) which are used in a Japanese room like the European French window, and the solid inside sliding doors that divide one room from another. The literal meaning of *shōji* is "interceptor" and it was first used for any sort of screen, whether sliding or standing independently. The sliding variety was known as *fusuma-no-shōji*, and the meaning of *fusuma* is "bed-quilt," a name that was given to this kind of sliding door because the pattern on it originally was like that on a bed-quilt. The word *shōji* was then dropped and these inside doors were known as *fusuma* only, and also *karakami* or Chinese paper from the material with which they were covered. The standing screen of one leaf, which was used in the Heian period before there were any sliding doors, was called *tsuitate-no-shōji*, and in the same way the word *tsuitate* is now used by itself to denote a single-leaf screen. The word *shōji* was then left to denote what took the place of the old *shitomi* or flap-gratings covered with paper, still seen in Shinto shrines and temples. The papered *shōji* is only a very much lighter version of this with wide spaces and very thin and delicate slats. The early *shōji*, as in the first half of the Ashikaga period, were only papered on their upper part, the lower being solid wood, the *koshitaka-shōji* or waist-high variety still used in kitchens. Actually they are already found in the Hakuzan shrine at Uji of the Kamakura period. A later development was to paper the whole of it to give a greater amount of light in the reception and other rooms. It was lighter in weight, too, and would slide more easily, and this quality no doubt also caused the heavy wooden sliding doors to be replaced by paper covered *fusuma*. The construction of the frames of both is much the same, but the *fusuma* is papered on both sides with thick paper. The wooden sliding door or *mairado* is still used for cupboards and other places. No doubt these heavy wooden fittings were more to the liking of the tough Kamakura warriors than to the elegant companions of the Ashikaga Shoguns, and it may be that the progress of the craft of paper-making had something to do with it.

THE CEILING

The commonest and simplest ceiling in Japanese houses is the flat one made of thin boards overlapping at the edges and laid over slender transverse rods or beams, the whole being suspended by perpendicular ties that attach it to the rafters above. It is called *saobuchi-tenjo* (rod ceiling) or, when the beams are bevelled, *saruho-tenjo* (monkey-cheek ceiling). Though extremely light and cohesive and so safe from falling in earthquakes, it has the defects that the boards are apt to curl and chinks open; the rats commit a nuisance through it and dust accumulates there, coming down, especially in an old house, like rain in a high wind. Also when the thatch has to be renewed in a thatched house this settlement of dust is particularly troublesome. And at night when the rats begin to scamper about they are apt to shake down this dust in the faces of people sleeping underneath.

The coffered ceiling, if well constructed, is not liable to these defects. It was common in the early days and came from China, but was more or less confined to temples and large residences. The ordinary house, which for long remained unceiled, never adopted the coffered ceiling but took to the simpler variety. The Japanese word for ceiling, *tenjo* (heaven's well), refers to the coffered type, for the squares on it are like the Chinese character for a well-head. The ceilings of tea-rooms are different in that they are often made of plaited wood or bamboo strips or of reeds, and the supporting rods are often bamboos also. Small though they are, tea-rooms not seldom have three varieties of ceiling together. The formal which is the Saobuchi type, the intermediate, of reeds etc. at a lower level, and the informal, consisting of the dressed open rafters (*kesho yane-ura*) which may be, for instance, of natural wood and bamboo alternating. But these conceits are not found elsewhere, except perhaps in a restaurant, where the uncommon and even bizarre is permissible because people do not have to live with it but only stay there for an hour or two. Generally speaking ceilings are uniform everywhere.

The reason why ceilings are rarely papered is the presence of those dwellers above them, the rats, that "are apt to do an unseemly peony on them." On this subject the famous comic poet, Shoku Sanjin, made the well-known couplet:

> *Nezumime ga Tenjo-bito no mane wo shite*
> *Shita-tare taruru Shii no Shōsho.*
> (These beastly rats are imitating courtiers
> Dropping down thus on a major-general of the Fourth Rank.)

which he composed to console a certain Daimyo who held the rank aforesaid when a rat urinated through the ceiling and spoiled his fine *shita-tare* or Court robe just as he was preparing to go and pay a visit in full dress at the Shogun's castle. There are two puns in this verse, the first *tenjo-bito* (courtiers) which could also be read "ceiling people," i.e. rats; and *shita-tare* which means both "a Court robe" and also "to drop down." However, in spite of this, ceilings are occasionally papered and decorated with writing or painting. Even the ordinary ceiling varies considerably in its value according to the fineness and evenness of the grain of the wood used in it. The grain must match and run in the same direction, so that the boards for one room must be cut from the same log.

CHAPTER XIV

PRIVY AND BATHROOM

THE PRIVY

THE privy in a Japanese house is sometimes under the same roof as the other rooms near the bathroom and sometimes built out under a roof of its own, either at the end of the veranda or else at a little distance and connected by a covered way. Never, I think, does it stand like a sentry-box looking self-conscious and far from ornamental, as it is apt to do in unsewered areas in Europe. It is always architecturally part of the house, and the woodwork and finish of it should be equal to the best elsewhere. As it is often said, "the *tokonoma* and the privy need the best work." This is doubtless because guests use it and is also a legacy from the Zen point of view on the subject, which is especially apparent in that attached to tea-rooms. The Japanese are, it may be noted, quite lacking in that latrinophobia which characterized the nineteenth century English.

The privy has an oblong slot in the floor edged with a porcelain or celadon fitting, and underneath this is a large jar let into the ground and cemented round about, perhaps a couple of feet below the floor. This is cleaned out through an opening in the wall beside it at intervals by the peasant whose privilege it is to remove the contents to fertilize his ricefields. Next to this compartment, which is technically called Daibenjo or Great Convenience Place, there is another containing a urinal which is called Shombenjo, the Lesser Convenience Place. These two conveniences are always catered for separately in this way, no doubt in the interests of agriculture. In restaurants and elegant houses these places are extremely tasteful and in the former case may often have a miniature garden or arrangement of rocks to adorn them. It is not perhaps an ideal arrangement, but it has worked well for centuries and presumedly will continue to do so. A Japanese critic says: "There are three ways apparently of solving this problem. That of the European who goes to great trouble and expense to remove and destroy what is very valuable fertilizer. That of the Japanese who conserves it and builds a suitable and seemly place in the house to do so. And that of the Chinese who spends nothing and provides nothing, but goes out into his garden and applies it directly. Logically the last is the most economical and effective, but——" The oldest word for privy is Kawaya, which is found in the *Kōjiki* and so is not later than the eighth century anyhow, of which more than one explanation is possible. It may be for "river-house," for there is evidence that in early days these conveniences were built over a stream as they are in the Koya temples where examples may still be seen. It may be noted that these passages in the *Kōjiki* refer to the Deities of Izumo where it is quite likely the whole house was often built over the water, and examples of this are to be found in the Naka-umi lagoon of that province still.

In the section of Jimmu Tenno we read that the Great God Onamuji had changed himself into a red painted arrow and so projected himself into the channel under the privy where a beautiful damsel was. She took it home and put it by her bed and it turned into a handsome youth and so she came to bear a daughter to the Deity. Incidentally thieves not seldom enter houses this way with no necessity for any metamorphosis. Another view is that Kawaya means "side-house" because it was built out under a separate roof. Or again the word *kawa* (excreta), is explained when it is a parallel with Hi-dono or gutter-chamber. The Hi-dono was a place where wooden vessels for use as a commode were kept and used and afterwards cleansed. The word for such a vessel is still *o-kawa*. This was the style of convenience in use in the palace and in great mansions, it would appear. The maid-in-waiting who looked after it was called Mi-kawa-yōdo Hisumashi (August-flushing-maid-in-waiting). That the greatest care was taken about its cleanliness is evident from some other names for this place, e.g. Seiyōsho or Pure Clean Place and also Setsuin, the classical word, first written up over the Tōsu of the Zen temple of Kenninji at Kyoto. It is compounded of *setsu*, part of the name of a Chinese monk who found enlightenment in cleaning it out, and *-in*, part of the name of his temple.

In the sixteenth century we have a detailed description of the Go-kansho or Retirement Place of Takeda Shingen the shrewd and ferocious Lord of Kai, famous both as a soldier and a scholar. It had an area of six mats (9 by 12 feet), so that Shingen would have plenty of room to manoeuvre if attacked there suddenly, a thing by no means unknown in those days when no scruples were observed. The drain from the bathroom next to it was led beneath it in order to utilize the waste water, so that Shingen, beside his other remarkable qualities, may also be the Japanese Harington. There was also a censer there in which fine incense was kept burning day and night by the gentlemen-in-waiting always on duty. And there Shingen had his state papers taken and would consider his decisions, and that may have been why he himself called it Yama, the mountain—of meditation.

THE BATHROOM

Bathrooms in residences are comparatively ancient, for there is one in the Seiryōden in the palace at Kyoto, while later on they are found in the great Zen temples and in the plans of the Kamakura military mansions. Some think that the steam bath such as is found in Hideyoshi's bathroom is the more ancient form and this may be so,[1] though hot spring baths were known and used in the tenth century (e.g. that of Dōgō in Shikoku) and hot water seems the simpler. There are no very early details perhaps, but it seems that the bathroom has not altered much since the sixteenth century.

There is a mention of a "plank bath" (*ita-buro*) in a story in the *Ima Monogatari* of about 1250, in which it is related that a monk who has some eye complaint goes to one with his eyes bandaged, and never having seen this kind of bath before mistakes a door in the street for it and proceeds to undress there, much to the amusement of the bystanders whose laughter leads him to take off the bandage and discover himself standing naked in the street.

The oldest type of bath seems to be one with an iron bottom on to which a coopered tub with bamboo bands was fitted. The bottom was set in a clay base like that of the kitchen stove and a fire of brushwood lit under it. To protect the feet from the hot bottom a wooden lid was floated on the water and the bather got on to this so that it sank with him. As the smoke was considerable, this kind of bath was usually put in an outhouse near the kitchen. It is known as Goemon-buro or

---

[1] There is also a very fine specimen at the Tōfukuji monastery illustrated in Amanuma's *Nippon Kenchikushi Zuroku*.

Goemon bath, from the highwayman Ishikawa Goemon who was boiled in one by Hideyoshi's orders and who made a long and defiant oration from it during the process. Some twenty years ago they still existed in the country and may still do so. Another type, probably later, is that in which there is a stove built into the bath tub, which is oval in section, so that the water circulates round it like a water tube boiler. A third type has the water heated in a detached furnace and boiler outside, which communicates with the bath by pipes. This is the kind generally used in hotels and public bath houses.

The hot spring bath houses at fashionable spas are often very fine buildings that might easily be mistaken for temples, with massive and lofty tiled roofs and very imposing entrances. Others are more of the farm-house type and blend very happily with the lines of the hills and sea shore. When Japanese bathe they like to get a good view at the same time, if at all possible, and so large windows will be placed in such a way that one can sit in the bath and look out on the hills or sea. The same thing applies also to hotels which are built facing a sea view, if by the shore, or country or garden one, if inland. This may not seem very remarkable, and yet in this city of Sydney of more than a million inhabitants, set round a piece of water that is not unknown in the world, there is perhaps hardly more than one hotel or restaurant where a meal can be combined with a sea view, even at one of the well-known bathing resorts on the coast. And one of the finest sites on the harbour is used as a tramway depot, though to lend it dignity it is disguised architecturally as a fortress. It is rather reminiscent of the armoured knight in the Victorian baronial hall whose belly opened to disclose a stove. Precisely the antithesis of these things is the town planning and building of Japan.

CHAPTER XV

THE KITCHEN

THE kitchen in a Japanese house naturally varies as elsewhere with the style and size of the building. In the country house and farm it is spacious and the boarded portion is often used as a family dining-room. It is always open to the roof to prevent stuffiness from the fumes of charcoal or faggots from the stove and braziers. It is neatly and efficiently arranged for convenient access to the vessels and utensils needed for cooking and serving meals, and here it is likely that it was influenced by the Mizuya or Tea-kitchen of the ceremonial tea-room where every utensil has its exact place, thought out to conform with the principle of economy of movement, which is one of the main features of ceremonial tea-serving. So the kitchen is always next or very close to the family living-room, bathroom and servant's room, and the isolation of these parts of the residence as incompatible with "gentility" has never come about and does not need to be corrected as in modern European styles. This is largely because the servants are all maids and are treated as members of the family. The custom was and still is that members of the social grade just one below that of the family should be employed as domestics, beginning with the Court where daughters of the Court nobility served, and the mansions of the Shogun where those of the lesser military nobles and Samurai were employed.

In the kitchen the stove is an important object, regarded with deep respect or veneration as the source of sustenance for the house.[1] It had its tutelary Deity, like the well and the privy and the garden. Where this stove was in the covered court by the kitchen there was in the northern provinces a big odd-vizaged figure as much as six feet

---

[1] The phrase *"Kamado wo tateru,"* (to set up a stove) means "to begin house-keeping," just as *"Noren wo wakeru"* (to split the shop curtain) means "to start a separate shop."

high up against the pillar against which the stove was placed. This was called the male pillar (*otoko-bashira*) and the figure, *hyōtoku*, which Fujita conjectures to be the same as *hyottoko*, the common word for "an ugly fellow," possibly from *hi-otoko* (fire male). Kōshin is usually the kitchen Deity, and food and drink offerings are made before him. Sometimes it seems the breakfast rice is cooked with fire lighted from the sacred flame that burns before his shrine.

The stove is built up of clay plastered over much like the setting of a copper and has sometimes one large or three, five, seven, or even nine smaller fireplaces in it, each with a hole on top on which the pot or cauldron is placed or, in the case of the large variety, inset. In Edo the stove is placed facing the earth floor of the kitchen, but in central Japan it faces the boarded part. In this region round the ancient capital the stove is also regarded as part of the house, even more so than the *shōji* and *fusuma*, whereas in Edo it is removed by the owner if he lets his house and the tenant must bring his own. In the extreme north climate has modified the kitchen, since there the open hearth, over which the pots are hung by a *jizai*[2] or suspender, has superseded the stove.

Though the stoves are often now made in a straight line, an old form that is still common in the country is the semicircular shape, by which the fire and cooking vessels are brought within easy reach of the cook without need of superfluous movement. In some old country houses there is one large stove that is unused and regarded as the sacred fireplace, while the cooking is done on a separate range. Mention of this reverence for the stove is found in the earliest records of the Nara age in the proceedings of the Palace Kitchen Department (Oi-ryo), and such observance may have derived from China where it is ancient enough, for we find in *Analects* iii, 13 the question "Is it better to pay attention to the God of the Hearth than to the ancestral shrine?" The *Li Ki* observes that the House Deity lives in the kitchen in spring, in the gate in summer, in the well in autumn and in the garden in winter. Fujita sees a reference to this in the kitchen god he found revered in parts of Okayama province, called Odokū Sama, which he interprets as the Japanese Tsuchi-gimi or Earth Lord.

---

[2] *Jizai* means literally "as you please," in reference to its adjustability.

CHAPTER XVI

THE ARCHITECT

THE architect in the sense that we now understand the word, that is a scholarly professional expert who can design anything in any style to order, has really only been known in Japan since the Restoration of 1868 and the introduction of European ways; but the history of the constructive craftsman and artist, professional and amateur, is not so very different from what we find elsewhere. As the arts and crafts entered Japan with Buddhism it was natural that Buddhist monks and scholars should be the experts in them and the directors of construction, for they had knowledge and leisure and were able to travel on the continent. That they should have remained so was only to be expected, for right up to the seventeenth century professional men like doctors and Chinese scholars and painters were all tonsured, though that is probably as far as the religious aspect of the majority went. Zen monks were the fathers of domestic architecture and gardening, as we have seen, and they in turn produced the Tea Master who continued where they left off and became an hereditary professional aesthete in a very specialized sense. One great advantage that a monk possessed, even a nominal one, was that he was outside all social grades, since theoretically he did not belong to the world at all, and so was free to enter any society no matter how exalted, even that of "Those Above the Clouds," where only the highest Court noble might go.

In the earliest days there was the monk Dōji of the Sanron sect who studied in China for sixteen years (701-717). He brought plans from the Hsi Ming temple in China which he used to build the Daianji, one of the seven great temples of Nara. Similarly Gembo of the Hosso sect and Kanshin, Chinese monks, came to Japan and worked in the same era.

Quite as important as the designer was the craftsman or temple builder, Zōjiko ("make temple artisan"), also called Daitōryō (master carpenter), or simply Takumi (craftsman). He and his associated assistants did the work, and the skill they must already have possessed, judging from the workmanship of the most ancient objects, evidently enabled them to carry out anything required of them. Since the technique of wood-working does not alter, the country has always retained a large population of these artisans living simply and inexpensively, yet able to do fine work, and, owing to their long apprenticeship and hereditary craft, endowed with an eye naturally sensitive to harmony of form and balance.

Since Zen monks were even more secular in their ways than the other kinds and particularly cultivated a simple and functional manner of living as likely to lead to enlightenment, they studied the layout and details of buildings and gardens. Scholarly and versatile indeed, they would do anything for the great feudal lords, their patrons and often relatives, from planning their gardens and family temples to carrying on their dubious diplomacy when it seemed profitable and even sometimes leading their armies when it ceased to be so.

So when Hideyoshi had restored something like peace after the many wars of the sixteenth century and began to build temples and palaces, it was a monk of Mount Koya he put in charge of his works. This Mokujiki Shōnin is described as having been in charge of the buildings on Mount Koya since he was twenty-five years old and very experienced; and when Hideyoshi's great Buddha temple was being raised he built himself a little hut beside the work and did not leave it day or night. He became a great friend and confidant of the art-loving autocrat and was one of the very few permitted to attend his quiet funeral.

The Tea Master had already begun to act in the latter half of the Ashikaga period as aesthetic advisor to the Shogun and his nobles, and in their days his sphere was limited to them and to the details of etiquette. But with the rise of the famous Sen Rikyu in the days of Nobunaga and Hideyoshi, the Tea Master's influence spread to the military men and merchants and the ordinary people, and definitely affected architecture.[1]

The Tea Master was like an architect who was given a commis-

---

[1] The spirit of the Tea Master as expressed in pottery is revealed in a masterly way, by Bernard Leach in his charming volume, *A Potter's Book* recently published.

sion to design a house with its interior decoration, furniture and garden, as well as to instruct the owner how to live in it properly. He became the arbiter of taste and the critic of pottery and pictures and stones and bamboos and all the other things that make life in the opinion of cultured Japanese. And since, like all the other arts and crafts, his business became an hereditary one and branched out all over the country, it helped to keep taste at a higher level through the Tokugawa period than might otherwise have been the case. The house of Sen Rikyu still flourishes and now in the fourteenth generation remains unique in the aristocracy of aestheticism.

Among these Tea Masters the most famous for his creations in building and garden planning was Kobori Masakazu (1579-1647), usually known as Kobori Enshu because his title was Lord of Tōtōmi, which is commonly abbreviated thus. His family was a military one and he had an income of 10,000 *koku* per annum, while he acted as Chief of the Board of Works for the Shogun's mansion and also as Commissioner of Fushimi, an administrative position in the government. He was distinguished in all the arts, painting and poetry, flowers and tea, and connoisseurship of antiques. Very many fine gardens are ascribed to him, and as he was the teacher of the Shogun Iemitsu for tea and his advisor on art matters generally, none had more influence in these things, especially as Iemitsu was an enthusiastic art patron as well as a great autocrat. He was in some sort a Japanese edition of Sir John Vanbrugh born a few decades after his death, but the light and delicate work he has left is as great an antithesis to the massive ostentation of the latter as well can be. The retired Emperor Go-Mizu-no-ō, who died in 1680 aged eighty-five, was also a great expert in building and garden planning as well as a distinguished man of letters.

Since the work of a Japanese building can so safely be left to the master carpenter and is so largely standardized, it is very easy to be an amateur architect, and their number has always been large. Particularly do retired people, whose hobby is often Chanoyu, interest themselves in building or rebuilding parts of their houses and making tea-rooms and gardens. And though the buildings are standardized in their measurements there is plenty of variety in detail and in the arrangement of the buildings on the site and the relation of the rooms to the gardens Since there is no finality about the building of a

Japanese house, and it is not a squarish block dumped on the middle, or at one end, of a piece of land, there is always opportunity for amusement for the owner and the carpenter in adding another section or a detached room in the garden.

Mention should be made, too, of the famous artist Honami Kō-etsu, whose pottery and lacquer are so well known even in the West, and who is renowned in Japan as one of the greatest calligraphists and artists. He designed and laid out a village for himself and all his craftsmen to live in, on a charming site at Takagamine outside Kyoto. There was no art in which he did not excel; indeed, he was an amateur of them all, for his profession was that of hereditary sword connoisseur to the government, for which he was paid quite a comfortable salary.

Later on, about 1800, there was the Daimyo Matsudaira Fumai, lord of the province of Izumo, the most outstanding figure among the feudal nobles of his day, who was not only a very able administrator of his fief but a great Tea Master and connoisseur and writer on aesthetic matters. He was a fine amateur architect and designed his garden at Ozaki outside Tokyo with its numerous detached villas and tea-rooms.[2] He was blessed with a master carpenter named Kobayashi Jōdei, of extraordinary skill, who was quite a wizard in any kind of woodwork and in Europe would no doubt have been called a great sculptor. In Japan he was just an artisan, eccentric in his behaviour and a great toper, but otherwise quite content to carry out his master's designs.

It was Matsudaira Fumai who restored and added to the Kōhōan villa in the Zen temple of Daitokuji at Kyoto, built by Kobori Enshu as a retreat for his retirement. This great monastery is the Pantheon of eminent aesthetes, many of them dictators and statesmen as well, and most of their memorial chapels are worth a visit.

The hereditary master carpenter to the Shoguns, Kōra Buzen-no-kami or Lord of Buzen had a nobleman's title, a privilege he shared with all swordsmiths whose craft was naturally the most appreciated; but these were honours only and carried with them no noble status or income. And practically all buildings were built by these craftsmen,

---

[2] *Vide* the author's monograph on him in the 25th Anniversary Volume of the Meiji Japan Society, Tokyo, 1937.

supervised on occasions by their employers or by some Tea Master or amateur aesthete.

So the reason why in Japan an architect can be dispensed with, and yet the labour of the builders be not in vain, is primarily because Japanese structures are put up with a view not to their outside appearance but to their function. The roof is the only part that may be impressive. It may be noted, too, that there is no monumental architecture in Japan—with some exceptions that are copies of Occidental work. No statuary is found commemorating the great, though the longest avenue in the world was planted in honour of one of them. The tombstone is but a neat slab to hold an inscription and the great lord had only a conventional stupa. Imperial tombs are natural hills overgrown with trees. The idea of calling great men or events to remembrance by useless and expensive piles of stone has not occurred to the Japanese. Neither have gardens ever contained statuary or fountains consisting of figures that vomit water. This latter seems quite a Western idiosyncrasy, for neither India nor China nor even Egypt knows of it.

The landscape garden with its conventionalized natural scenery is really a more important part of the composition than the house, since the latter is but the shelter from the weather from which to look at it. So it follows that a garden planner is more essential than an architect, for when the garden is made the craftsman has only to put the house into it as seems most fitting. This process must, of course be modified in crowded streets and business premises, in which the courtyard gardens are apt to be embraced by the buildings; but the feeling is not different. It is, in fact, the garden maker who is really the architect, who "adds use to beauty and space to strength," but not by any means the gardener. He has nothing to do with it, and thus the result is very much the antithesis of the builder's house in the seed-shop gardener's garden that practically without exception greets the eye in this island continent. For the Japanese garden is made to supply shade and coolness and privacy and quiet, as well as a living picture from the house through the whole year; it is not a small nursery or a place for the competitive growing of flowers.

APPENDIXES

APPENDIX I

PROFESSOR AMANUMA'S *ILLUSTRATIONS OF JAPANESE ARCHITECTURE (NIPPON KENCHIKUSHI ZUROKU)*

THIS appendix contains the page numbers and list of plates in Professor Amanuma's *Illustrations of Japanese Architecture (Nippon Kenchikushi Zuroku)*. It may serve the double purpose of identifying the photographs in the four volumes of this work for those who wish to consult it but do not read Japanese, and also of providing a comprehensive list of historic Japanese buildings according to their successive epochs.

ASUKA PERIOD
(552–645)

	Page	
VOL. I	3	Izumo shrine
	4	Sumiyoshi shrine
	5	Ise great shrine, Honden
	6	Atsuta shrine
	7	Hōryuji temple
	8	Middle gate and pillar bases
	9	side view
	10	eaves
	11	balustrade
	12–13	Kondo
	14	stylobate
	15	eaves
	16–19	details of roof
	20–3	bracketing
	24	doors
	25	interior brackets
	26	balustrade
	27	Pagoda
	28–9	altar details
	30–1	pinnacle
	32–3	balustrade
	34–5	spire and finial
	36–9	Cloister
	40–3	roof details
	44–7	Shitennōji, Osaka
	48–9	Kondo
	50	Hokkiji, pagoda
	51	Eaves

Page
52   Hōrinji, pagoda
53   Eaves and finial tile
54–5   Stone pagodas, Sakuragawa village, Shiga prefecture
56–65   Hōryuji, Tamamushi shrine

NARA PERIOD
(645–794)
Early Period, 645-709

68–73   Kairyuōji, model pagoda
74–7   Yakushiji, pagoda

Later Period, 709–794

        Tōdaiji
90–1   Reconstruction of Nandaimon
92   cloister
93   pagoda
94   middle gate
95   Buddha hall
96   Tengai gate
97–111   details of brackets roofs and tiles
112   Hokkedo
113–19   details of roofs brackets and altar base
120–1   Library
122–3   Shōsōin, treasure-house
124–9   Shin-Yakushiji, Hondo
130–1   Kairyuōji, Sai Kondo
132–41   Toshōdaiji, Kondo
142–3   Kōdō (lecture hall)
144–7   Hōryuji, east gate
148–51   Library
152–7   Refectory and loggia
158–61   Tōin Dempōdō
162–5   Yumedono
166–7   Taimadera
168–71   East and west pagodas
172–5   Eisanji, octagonal hall (Hakkaku-endo)
176   Internal roof construction
177–9   Designs on canopy and tie-beams
180–7   Stupa carvings, stone stupas, pillar bases and stone finial tiles of this period

HEIAN PERIOD
(794–1185)
Early Period, 794–897

190–4   Murōji, pagoda
195–200   Kondo
206   Mount Koya, site of great pagoda

Page
207   Negoroji Dai Dempōin, pagoda (rebuilt 1515)
208   *Right,* Metal Yugi pagoda, Hōryuji
      Left, Yugi pagoda stupa shrine, Manseiji temple,
          Togano, Osaka
209   Picture of Yugi Daishi, Ryukoin temple, Mount Koya
210   Yugi pagoda rebuilt at Ryukoin, Mount Koya, by
          Professor Amanuma
211   Sorinto at Enryakuji, Hieizan

Later Period, 897–1185

214   Daigōji, pagoda
215–22   Details and decoration of Ohara Sansenin temple, Hondo
223–5   Ōjō Gokurakuin
226–61   Hōōdo of Byōdōin Uji
262–7   Amidadō of Hokkaiji
268–70   Joruri-dera, Hondo
271–3   Yaku-shido of Kami-daigo temple
274–9   Hōryuji, Saiin belfry
280–5   Daikōdō
286–93   Kakurinji, Daishido
294–5   Jōkōdō
296–9   Hakusui, Amidadō
300–1   Kōzōji, Amidadō
302–7   Chusonji, Konjikidō
308–9   Fukutokuan, Hondo (Nagano)
310–13   Sambutsuji, Nageiridō
314–15   Fukiji, Daidō
316–18   Wall paintings at Kōchi before and after restoration
319   Yakushidō
320–3   Stone stupas
324–5   Demon tiles
326–7   Kasuga shrine, Nara
328–9   Usa shrine
330   Kamo shrine, Kyoto
331   Hiyoshi shrine, Sakamoto
332   Uji shrine

KAMAKURA PERIOD
(1185–1392)
Wayo Style

VOL. II   1–71   Rengeō-in, Hondo (Sanjusangen-dō)
          72–83   Kyō-ō Gokokuji (Tōji), details
          84–5   east gate of Kanchoin
          86–7   log built treasury
          88–93   Daihonji, Hondo
          94–7   Nembutsuji, Hondo
          98–105 Daigōji, Kondo
          106–9   Iwabunedera, pagoda (3 story)

Page
110–15   Kumihama Hongwanji, Hondo
116–27   Kōdaiji, pagoda (Tahōtō)
128–31   Kaijusanji, pagoda (4 story)
132–3   Monju hall
134   Hōjōji, Nio gate
135   Hondo and covered water tank
136–7   Interior shrine
138–52   Daifukkōji, Hondo
153–8   Pagoda (Tahōtō)
160–5   Byōdōin, Kwannon hall
166–9   Gokurakuin, Hondo
170–2   Kōfukuji, Hokuendo
173   Hōryuji, Saiendo
174–5   Jūrinin, Hondo
176   Tōdaiji, Hokkedo
177–9   Akadana (projecting ablution chamber)
180   Reido (prayer hall)
182–7   Ai-no-ma (middle chamber)
188–9   Chozuya (washing place)
190–1   Shin Yakushiji, east gate
192–3   Bell-tower
194–6   Toshōdaiji, drum tower
197   Shariden and Reido (reliquary and prayer hall)
198–201 Yakushiji, Tōindo
202–13   Chōkyuji
214–25   Hōryuji, Seirenin
226–7   Sankyoin
228–34   Toin, Shariden (reliquary)
235   painted chamber
236–7   Chōgakuji, Gochido
234–49   Taimadera, Mandara hall
250–1   Murōji, Kanchodo, before and after restoration
252–5   Kondo
256   Daiyakuji, Hondo
257   Daishido
258–9   Enjōji, pagoda (3 story)
260–7   Ishiyamadera, pagoda (Tahōtō)
268–74   Saimyōji of Ikedera (Kora village, Shiga prefecture)
275–7   Kongorinji, Hondo
278–87   Kōōnji, Kwannon hall
288–91   Jiganin, Kondo (Hineno village, Osaka)
292–7   Pagoda (Tahōtō)
298–307 Shōjōin, Hondo
308–15   Kongo Sammaiin, Pagoda (Tahōtō) built by Masako, oldest
              Tahōtō with Ishiyama, 1222
316–19   Library (log built)
320–33   Kongobuji, Mount Koya, Fudo hall, 1197

Page

334–41   Chōhōji, Hondo
342–53   Pagoda (Tahōtō)
354–79   Mirokuji, Hondo (Sugano village, Hyogo prefecture)
380–9   Jōdōji, Hondo (Onomichi, 1226)
390–7   Pagoda (Tahōtō)
398–409   Daisanji, Hondo
410–11   Ishide temple, gate (near Dōgō hot spring, Iyo)
412–15   Pagoda (3 story)
416–17   Bell-tower
418–29   Hondo
430–3   Jōkaiji, Hondo (Inazawa village, Aichi prefecture)
434–7   Stupa shrine
438–41   Ryuzanji, gate (Tokiwa village, Aichi prefecture)
442–9   Hondo
450–1   Chusonji, Konjikido (Oido, 1120 and 1222)
452   Reizanji, Hondo
453   Toshōdaiji, Kōdō, altar
454–5   Hōdōji, altar (Ikoma village, Nara)
456   Tōdaiji, Hokkedo, shrine base
457   Shin Yakushiji, Hondo, altar
458–60   Kongoji, Hondo, pillar bases

Kara Style

VOL. III   1–13   Fusaiji, Buddha hall
            14–21   Umeda, Shaka hall
            22–35   Ankokuji, Shaka hall (Tomo Port.)
            36–51   Shinkakuji, Hondo (Nishi Ono village, Oita prefecture)
            52–61   Eihōji, Kwannon hall (Tajimi town, Toki district, Gifu
                        prefecture 1314)
            62–85   Kaisando
            86–93
            94–103 Tenonji, Buddha hall (built by Ashikaga Yoshimitsu, 1312
                        Toyotomi village, Takada district, Aichi prefecture)
            104–12 Suadera Ietomi town, Ashikaga, city Tochigi prefecture)

Tenjiku Style

114–33   Daigōji, Library
134–44   Tōdaiji, Nandaimon
145–52   Kaisando (Founder's hall called also Ryobendo or
                Ryoben hall from name of founder)
153–5   Bell-tower
156–70   Jōdōji Jōdō hall (Ono town, Hyogo prefecture)

Composite Style

172–8   Kanshinji, Hondo

Shinto Shrines

180–1   Tamate-yori-matsuri-kitaru-sakatoki shrine (log built house
                for the Sacred Car; Oyamasaki village, Kyoto prefecture)

Page
182–3   Hakusan shrine, Uji
184–9   Mitamaya shrine, Kamo, Kyoto
190–2   Uji Kami shrine, (upper shrine), Haiden
195   Uji main shrine
196–7   Saga shrine, Yamagi village Kyoto
198–207   frog-crotches
208–13   Enjōji Kasuga Hakusan shrine
214–15   Itsukushima shrine
216   Site of Eikyuji temple, Nara
217–27   Ishigami shrine, Haiden
228–37   Uda Mizuwake shrine, Kyoto
238–51   Shinra Zenshindo shrine
252–5   Mikami shrine (Shiga prefecture), Haiden
256   Gate
257–65   Honden
266–9   Kasuga shrine (Oishi village, Omi)
270–1   Ono shrine (Konze village, Shiga prefecture), gate
272–4   Oshidate shrine (Shiga prefecture)
275–86   Tate Mizuwake shrine (Akasaka village, Osaka)
287–95   Sakurai shrine (Niwatani village, Osaka prefecture)
296–303   Jōdōji temple, Hachiman shrine, Haiden
304–5   Itsukushima shrine, Marōdō shrine, Harai-dono
306–16   Honden
317–78   Stone pagodas, stupa pagodas, reliquaries and pillars
380–91   Demon-faced finials
393–5   Futaiji temple (Nara), south gate
396–406   Giant frog-crotch

MUROMACHI PERIOD
(1362–1570)

VOL. IV   3–6   Kaenji Kinkakuji, Kyoto
          7–10   Gishōji, Ginkakuji, Kyoto
          11–12   Tōkyudo
          13–17   Manjuji, Aizen hall, Kyoto
          18–21   After typhoon of 1934
          22–9   Tōfukuji temple, Sammon gate
          30–9   Inner decoration of Sammon gate
          40–9   Tōsu or Necessarium
          50   Bath house, exterior
          51–6   interior
          54–5   vapour baths
          57–8   Hōtōji temple, Kyoto, pagoda (Tahōtō)
          59–65   Suonan temple, Tanabe (Kyoto), Hondo
          66–9   Enjōji (Yagyu village, Nara), gate
          70–1   Hōryuji, gate
          72–3   Tōin, cloister
          74–6   Zuika-in temple, Hirano village, Nara
          77–87   Kimbu-senji temple, Yoshino

Page
88–97   Fudōji temple (Shimoda village, Shiga prefecture), Hondo
98–101   Chōhōji temple (Hamanaka village, Wakayama), gate
102–5   Hōonji temple (Iwakura village, Wakayama), Hondo
106–13   Yakushi hall
114–21   Dai-Dempo-in (Negoro, Wakayama), pagoda (Tahōtō)
122–37   Kakurinji temple, Hondo
138–9   Altar
140–5   Shrine eaves
146–54   Jōdōji temple, Hondo
155–61   Shrine details
162–77   Myōō-in temple (Kusado village, Hiroshima prefecture)
178–97   Fudō-in temple (Ushida village, Hiroshima prefecture)
198   Kōjōji temple (Setoda town, Hiroshima prefecture)
199–209   Pagoda (3 story), 1442
210–17   Tōzenji temple (Hiyoshi village, Imaharu, Ehime prefecture),
             Yakushi hall
218–21   Shrine
222–7   Kōryuji temple, Hondo
224–5   Peculiar capitals
228–9   Sempukuji temple (Toyosaki village, Oita prefecture),
             Kaisando
230   Jōkōji temple (Shinano village, Aichi prefecture) Hondo
231–5   Altar
236–45   Anrakuji temple (Bessho village, Nagano prefecture), pagoda
             (octagonal)
246–9   Taihōji temple (Urasato village, Nagano prefecture),
             Kwannondo shrine
250–3   Kokubunji temple, pagoda (3 story)
254–60   Enshōji temple (Miyoshi village, Nagano prefecture),
             Shaka hall
261–3   Altar
264–5   Pagoda shrine, 1502
266–71   Enyūji temple (Hikin town, Tokyo prefecture), Hondo
272   Jizo hall (Hibashi village, Fukushima prefecture)

Shinto Shrines
274–83   Daigoji temple, Seiryudo, Haiden
280–1   Shitomi and early *shōji*
284–93   Kuse shrine, Kyoto
294–7   Suido shrine (Terada village), Kyoto
298–315 Soraku shrine (Soraku village, Kyoto), friezes and
             frog-crotches
316–21   Danzan shrine, Sakurai pagoda (only wooden 13-story
             pagoda in Japan)
322–5   Monjuin Hakusando (Abe village, Nara prefecture)
326–41   Jishu shrine (Katsuragawa village, Shiga prefecture)
342–6   Katte shrine (Kagamigawa village, Shiga prefecture)

Page

347–59   Yuhi shrine, (Yuhi village, Shiga prefecture), carved figures of dancers, 1493

360–3   Hachiman shrine (Ono village, Kyotani Hyogo prefecture), frog-crotches

364–9   Kibitsu shrine (Ichinomiya village, Okayama prefecture)

370–91   Itsukushima shrine (Hiroshima prefecture)

392–405   Ima-Hachiman shrine (Yamaguchi city)

406–17   Hachiman shrine (Hachiman village, Aichi prefecture)

418–27   Koshio shrine (Omagari town, Akita prefecture)

428–9   Hachiman shrine (Jogo village, Yamagata prefecture)

430–2   Dewa shrine (Toge village, Higashi-tagawa district, Yamagata prefecture), pagoda (5 story)

Devil-face Finial Titles, Inscriptions etc.

434–43   Hōryuji, Nandaimon tiles

MOMOYAMA AND EDO PERIODS
(1560–1600)

VOL. V   2   Kyōō Gōkokuji (Tōji) monastery, Nandaimon

          3   Nandaimon, side view

          4–7   gable

          8   Kondo

          9–12   details

          13–15   altar

          16   Hiunkaku villa, Nishi Hongwanji monastery

          17   Boat entrance

          18–19   Interior

          20   Dais chamber

          21   Corridor

          22   Bathroom shelf

          23   Entrance gable

          24   Great Hall of Audience

          25   dais

          26   dais alcove

          27   frieze

          30   Haku Shōin reception chamber, corridor

          31   dais

          32–5   details of dais

          36   Kuro Shōin reception chamber, exterior

          37   corridor

          38–9   irikawa

          40   interior

          41–5   shelves

          46–7   Kiyomizu temple

          48   Balustrade

          49   West gate

Page

           Daitokuji monastery
50–1   Imperial Envoy's gate
52–61   upper story details
62   Karamon gate
63–96   details
           Daigōji Temple
97   Imperial Envoy's gate
98–9   Samboin, front Shōin reception chamber
100   cool pavilion
101   pavilion ceiling
102–3   corridor of front Shōin
104–7   Shinden reception chamber, window, shelf, and frieze
108   Site of pagoda (now burnt)
109   Gotai hall (now burnt)
110–17   details
118   Kokubunji temple, Sendai, Yakushi hall
119–22   Details
123–6   Altar details
127–8   Matsushima, Gotai hall
129–33   Interior shrine
134   Zuiganji temple, Matsushima
135–9   Middle gate
140–1   Onari-mon (Shogun's gate)

           Zuiganji Temple, Matsushima
142–3   Main hall, porch
144–5   gable
146–7   side view
148–51   details
152–61   interior details
162–71   Outer corridor details
172–83   Main hall and details
184–7   Risshakuji temple (Yamadera village, Yamagata prefecture), middle hall and details

           Edo Period Temples
189–91   Kyōō Gōkokuji (Tōji) pagoda
192–6   Kiyomizu temple, Kyoto
197–9   Chionin temple, Sammon gate
200–1   upper story details
202–5   Nanzenji temple, Sammon gate
206–8   Mampukuji temple, front gate
209   Manjuin gate
210–17   Sammon gate
218–21   Tōdaiji temple, Daibutsu hall
220–4   Kongobuji temple (Mount Koya), Yakushi and Ihai halls
225   Yakushi hall, eaves
226–9   porch
230   ceiling
231–6   altar

Page
237   Sufukuji temple (Nagasaki), Sammon gate
238–43   Dai Ippo gate
244–51   Gōhō hall
252–63   Great hall
264   Fukuzaiji temple (Nagasaki), middle gate
265   Stone struts of middle gate
266–9   Front hall
270–88   Main hall
290   Shitennōji temple (Osaka), pagoda (blown down, 1934)
291   Tennōji temple (Shitaya, Tokyo), pagoda
292   Asakusa Kwannon temple (Tokyo), pagoda
293   Hōsenji temple (Nakano, Tokyo), pagoda
294–9   Zōzōji temple (Shiba, Tokyo), San Gedatsu gate
300–1   Rinnōji temple (Nikko), main hall
302–3   Sōrinto pillar
304–5   Chōshōji temple (Hirosaki), gate
306–16   Saishōin temple (Hirosaki), pagoda
317–20   Jionji temple (Daigo village, Yamagata prefecture)

Momoyama Period Shrines

322   Mizuwake shrine (Yoshino), gate
323–31   Main hall
332–9   Iido shrine (Kumoi village, Shiga prefecture), main hall
340–3   Itsukushima shrine, Miyajima subsidiary shrine
344–9   Hachiman shrine (Hakozaki), gate
350–4   Munakata shrine (Tajima village, Fukuoka prefecture),
                  main hall
355   Sumiyoshi shrine (Sumiyoshi, Fukuoka prefecture), main
                  hall
356–67   Hakuzan shrine (Handa town, Nagano prefecture)
368–82   Ozaki Hachiman shrine (Sendai city), main hall

Edo Period Shrines

384–7   Iwashimizu Hachiman shrine (Kyoto), hall of offerings
                  (Heiden)
388–93   Outer hall
394–5   Corridor interior
396–9   Kashiwabara shrine (Yamato), oratory (formerly the
                  Naiji-dokoro of the Imperial Palace, Kyoto)
400–2   Kashii shrine (Fukuoka), main hall
403–8   Iwakizan shrine (Iwaki village, Aomori prefecture), gate
409–12   Oratory

Torii of the Momoyama and Edo Periods

414–15   Hakozaki shrine
416–17   Itsukushima shrine, Miyajima
419   Omiwa shrine, Omiwa, Nara

Page

Edo Period Bridges

420–1   The Kure covered bridge at Usa Hachiman shrine, Kyushu

Edo Period Mausoleum Shrines

423   Tōshōgu shrine (Nikko), torii and front gate
424–5   Torii
426–33   Pagoda
434–5   Stone chamber, corridor detail
436–48   Western corridor details
450–67   Main hall
468–9   Taiyuin shrine (Nikko), main hall, interior
470–1   Kōka gate
472–3   Bronze gate of inner mausoleum
474–6   Stupa pagoda of inner mausoleum

Momoyama Period

478–81   The two stone mausolea before the inner shrine, Mount Koya

Momoyama and Edo Periods

484–504 Tiles

SUPPLEMENT

Nara Period to Edo Period
(725–1870)
Temples

	Page		Period
SUPPLE-	2–11	Yakushiji temple, eastern pagoda, details	Muromachi
MENT	12–21	Ichijōji temple, pagoda	Muromachi
	22–4	Jōruri temple, pagoda	Nara and Heian
	25	Kōryuji temple, Keiguin octagonal hall	Kamakura
	26–7	Tōfukuji temple, Gekka gate (from Imperial Palace)	Kamakura
	28–35	Jōdōji temple (Harima)	Kamakura
	36–47	Jōdōji temple (Onomichi), Amida hall and stupa pagoda	Kamakura
	48–67	Kōryuji temple, main hall	Muromachi
	68–71	Shakusonji temple (Kawabe village, Nagano), Amida hall and inner shrine	Heian
	72–5	Zensanji temple (Nishi Shiota village, Nagano), pagoda	Kamakura
	76–85	Hōtōji temple, gate and stupa pagoda	Muromachi
	86–99	Buttsuji temple (Takasaka village, Hiroshima prefecture), Jizo hall	Muromachi
	100–3	Dōshunji temple (Yamaguchi city), Kwannon hall	Muromachi
	104–11	Rurikōji temple (Yamaguchi city), pagoda	Muromachi
	112–13	Tōfukuji temple (Yamaguchi city), main hall	Muromachi
	114–25	Yakushi hall	Muromachi

126–137	Jōunji temple (Iwaki village, Ehime prefecture), Kwannon hall	Muromachi
138–145	Ankokuji temple (Kofu village, Gifu prefecture), library	Muromachi
146–158	Honkokuji temple (Kakinomoto town, Kyoto), library	Momoyama
159–167	Shomanin temple (Yuigaoka town, Osaka), stupa pagoda	Momoyama
168–175	Honkyoji temple (Amagasaki town, Hyogo prefecture), founder's hall	Muromachi
166–181	Shinnyodo temple (Kyoto), pagoda	Muromachi
182–193	Kurodani temple (Kyoto), Sammon gate	Edo
194–9	Ninnaji temple (Kyoto), pagoda	Edo
200–22	Shitennōji temple (Osaka), Kondo	Edo

HEIAN TO MOMOYAMA PERIOD
(800–1570)
Shrines

Page		Period
224–5	Uji-kami shrine, main hall	Heian
226–8	Ichijoji temple, Goho hall	Kamakura
229–31	Myoken and Benten halls	Kamakura
232–43	Furukuma shrine (Yamaguchi city)	Muromachi
244–63	Hirashimizu Hachiman shrine (Hirakawa village, Yamaguchi prefecture)	Muromachi
264–6	Soe-mikata-ni-imasu shrine (Tomio village, Nara prefecture)	Muromachi
267–9	Dazaifu shrine, Shiga shrine	Muromachi
270–5	Yugi shrine (Kurama village. Kyoto)	Momoyama
276–87	Suwo shrine (Hongo village, Nagano prefecture)	Momoyama
288–93	Itsukushima shrine, Miyajima Toyokuni shrine	Momoyama

MOMOYAMA AND EDO PERIODS
Detached Palaces

295–307	Nijo detached palace (Kyoto)	Momoyama
308–317	Katsura detached palace (Kyoto)	Momoyama
318–331	Shūgakuin detached palace (Kyoto)	Edo

Residences

333–9	Residence of Yoshimura Hikojiro	Momoyama
340–1	Residence of Furui Yoshiya (Kumadori village, Osaka)	Momoyama
342–3	Frieze of reception room in Jōdōin Temple, Uji	Momoyama
344–5	Frieze of reception room of residence of Motoide Tsuminosuke (Oi village, Ehime prefecture)	Edo

Tea-Rooms

347–50   Saihoji temple (Kyoto), Shonantei tea-room   Momoyama
351–62   Minase shrine (Shimamoto village, Osaka),
     tea-room   Edo

Castles

364–403   Himeji castle, Harima   Momoyama

Tiles

405–32

COMPARATIVE TABLE OF DATES

India		China		Korea		Japan	
B.C.							
663–543	Age of Buddha	551– 479	Confucius			660	Jinmu Tenno. Early period
322	Maurya Empire						
273	Asoka						
200	Indo Greek Rulers of Gandhara						
122	Chinese journey to India	20	Han dynasty	Three dynasties: Koguryu, Kudara, Silla			
A.D.							
20	Scythian Kushan dynasty						
120	Kanishka	221	Three kingdoms				
320	Gupta Empire Hindu renaissance						
405–11	Travels of Fa Hien in India	420	Wei dynasty. North and South kingdoms				
455	White Huns	581	Sui dynasty			540	Asuka period
606	Harsha Vardhana of Kanauj	618	T'ang dynasty			640	Hakuho period
629–45	Travels of Hiuen Tsang						
660	Rajput kingdoms						
						720	Tempyo period
				935	Koryu dynasty	780	Heian period
		907	Five kingdoms				
		960	Sung dynasty				
1175	Muhammedan Turkish kingdom of Delhi	1127	South Sung dynasty			1190	Kamakura period
		1206	Yuan dynasty			1340	Muromachi period
		1368	Ming dynasty	1392	Yi dynasty	1570	Azuchi-Momoyama period
1526	Mogul Timurids	1616	Ching dynasty				
						1616	Edo period

GLOSSARY OF ARCHITECTURAL TERMS

相間 *Ai-no-ma,* stone-floored chamber.

明障子 *Akari shōji,* translucent sliding door.

雨戸 *Amado,* rain door.

蟻頭 *Ari-gashira,* dove-tail (ant-head).

蟻溝 *Ari-mizo,* dove-tail socket (ant-channel).

校倉 *Aze-kura,* log-built storehouse.

四阿 *Azumaya,* hipped roof building.

便所 *Benjo,* privy.

暈 *Bokashi,* shading off.

佛壇 *Butsudan,* buddhist shrine.

佛殿 *Butsuden,* buddha hall.

屏風 *Byōbu,* folding screen.

千鳥破風 *Chidori hafu,* dormer.

違棚 *Chigaidana,* irregular shelves.

千木 *Chigi,* projecting rafters.

粽 *Chimaki,* tapering pillar.

帳臺 *Chōdai,* a curtained seat or bed.

勅使門 *Chokushi-mon,* Imperial Envoy gate.

中段 *Chudan,* middle dais.

中門 *Chumon,* middle gate.

臺所 *Daidokoro,* kitchen.

大工 *Daiku,* carpenter.

臺輪 *Daiwa,* wall plate.

大斗 *Daito,* pillar capital.

大塔 *Daito,* great stupa pagoda.

出丸 *Demaru,* barbican.

土臺 *Dōdai,* foundation stone.

土間 *Dōma,* earth floor.

海老虹梁 *Ebi kōryo,* lobster tie-beam.

海老束 *Ebi tsuka,* lobster brace.

緣側 *Engawa,* veranda.

吹寄棰   *Fuki-yose taruki*, clustered rafters.

袋棚   *Fukuro-dana*, hanging shelf.

舟肘木   *Funa hijiki*, boat-shaped elbow bracket.

風呂場   *Furoba*, bathroom.

風呂屋   *Furoya*, public bath house.

袋障子   *Fusuma shōji*, opaque sliding doors.

襖   *Fusuma*, opaque sliding doors.

蒲團   *Futon*, sleeping quilt.

伽藍   *Garan*, monastery (Samgharama).

外陣   *Gaijin*, outer sanctuary.

下段   *Gedan*, lower dais.

懸魚   *Gegyo*, verge-board (suspended fish).

玄關   *Genkan*, entrance hall.

擬寶珠   *Giboshi*, balustrade pillar-head.

五重塔   *Gōju-no-to*, five-story pagoda.

格天井   *Gō tenjo*, coffered ceiling.

破風   *Hafu*, gable.

拜殿   *Haiden*, oratory.

八角堂   *Hakkaku-do*, octagonal hall.

鼻隱   *Hana-kakushi*, beam nose cover.

梁   *Hari*, cross-beam.

梁間   *Harima*, depth of a building.

柱   *Hashira*, pillar.

法堂   *Hatto*, instruction hall.

瓶束   *Heisoku*, king post.

竈   *Hettsui*, kitchen stove.

肘木   *Hijiki*, elbow capital.

引手   *Hikite*, door push.

廣小舞   *Hiro-komai*, wide lath.

廂   *Hisashi*, a lean to.

檜皮葺   *Hiwada-buki*, hinoki shingled roof.

方形   *Hōgyo*, pyramidal roof.

方丈   *Hōjo*, monks' residence.

寶珠   *Hōju*, upper bulb on pagoda spire (pearl).

本殿   *Honden*, main shrine.

本瓦   *Hongawara*, true tile.

本丸   *Hon maru*, main ward of castle.

寶塔   *Hōtō*, small stupa pagoda.

枘   *Hōzō*, tenon.

井戸　　　*Ido*, well.
井桁　　　*Igeta*, well-head.
入側　　　*Irikawa*, matted corridor.
入母屋　　*Irimoya*, hipped-gable roof.
爐　　　　*Irori*, hearth.
板間　　　*Itama*, boarded floor.
板支輪　　*Ita shirin*, boarded soffit, or cove.
泉殿　　　*Izumi dono*, cooling pavilion.

地袋　　　*Jibukuro*, cupboard on the ground.
地貫　　　*Jinuki*, tie through base of pillar.
上段　　　*Jōdan*, upper dais.
城郭　　　*Jōkaku*, castle.
城下町　　*Jōka machi*, castle town.

壁　　　　*Kabe*, wall.
蟇股　　　*Kaerumata*, frog-crotch strut.
鏡板　　　*Kagami-ita*, large panel.
鏡天井　　*Kagami tenjo*, panelled ceiling.
廻廊　　　*Kairo*, cloister.
開山堂　　*Kaisando*, founder's hall.
筧　　　　*Kakehi*, gutter spout.
框　　　　*Kamachi*, frame or front beam, as of *tokonoma*.
竈　　　　*Kamado*, kitchen stove.
鴨居　　　*Kamoi*, grooved lintel.
要　　　　*Kaname*, hinge.
唐破風　　*Kara-hafu*, Chinese gable.
唐紙　　　*Karakami*, opaque sliding doors.
唐様　　　*Karayō*, Chinese style.
笠木　　　*Kasagi*, capping beam.
頭貫　　　*Kashira-nuki*, tie through head of pillar.
火頭窓　　*Kato-mado*, ogee arch headed window.
堅魚木　　*Katsuo-gi*, cross balk on shrine ridge.
厠　　　　*Kawaya*, privy.
茅葺　　　*Kaya-buki*, reed thatch.
建築師　　*Kenchikushi*, architect.
化粧屋根裏　*Kesho-yane-ura*, dressed roof lining.
桁　　　　*Keta*, beam or wall-plate.
桁行　　　*Keta-yuki*, frontage of building.
几帳　　　*Kicho*, curtain.

切目椽 *Kirime-en,* veranda with boards at right angels to building.

切妻 *Kiritsuma,* gable.

階 *Kizahashi,* staircase.

勾配 *Kobai,* slope of roof.

木鼻 *Kobana,* beam nosing.

拳鼻 *Kobushi-bana,* fist-shaped beam nosings.

柿葺 *Kokera-buki,* shingled roof.

小舞 *Komai,* laths under tiles or plaster.

金堂 *Kondo,* golden hall.

鼓樓 *Kōrō,* drum-tower.

虹梁 *Kōryo,* tie-beam.

腰障子 *Koshi-shōji,* half-panelled *shōji.*

腰貫 *Koshi-nuki,* tie through middle of pillar.

火燵 *Kotatsu,* quilt warming hearth.

小屋梁 *Koya-bari,* roof-beam.

小屋束 *Koya-tsuka,* roof tie.

釘隠 *Kugi-kakushi,* nail cover.

組入天井 *Kumi-iri tenjo,* grated ceiling.

雲方肘木 *Kumogata hijiki,* cloud-shape elbow bracket.

倉 *Kura,* fire-proof storehouse.

縁椽 *Kure-en,* veranda with boards parallel with house.

庫裏 *Kuri,* refectory kitchen of monastery.

刳形 *Kurigata,* moulding.

九輪 *Kurin,* nine-ringed pagoda spire ornament.

厨 *Kuriya,* kitchen.

櫛形 *Kushigata mado,* comb-shaped window.

経蔵 *Kyōzo,* sutra library.

疎棰 *Mabara-daruki,* rafters set wide apart.

舞良戸 *Mairado,* ribbed wooden sliding doors.

巻斗 *Makito,* bracket capital.

招屋根 *Maneki-yane,* lean-to continued over ridge (beckoning roof).

斗形 *Masugata,* pillar capital.

枡形 *Masugata,* castle gate.

迴椽 *Mawari-en,* veranda round a room.

門 *Mon,* gate.

物置 *Mono-oki,* store-room.

母屋 *Moya,* main building.

流造屋根   *Nagare-zukuri-yane*, continuation lean-to (cat-slide).
流   *Nagashi*, kitchen sink.
長押   *Nageshi*, frieze beam.
内陣   *Naijin*, inner sanctuary.
中坪   *Nakatsubo*, inner court.
海鼠瓦   *Namako-gawara*, convex joint-tile, imbrex "*bêche-de-mer*" tile.
海鼠壁   *Namako-kabe*, convex plaster joint of diagonal tiled wall.
納戸   *Nando*, bed-room, store-room.
根太   *Neta*, floor joist.
西丸   *Nishi maru*, western ward of castle.
野天上   *No-tenjo*, plain boarded ceiling.
軒   *Noki*, eaves.
軒唐破風   *Noki kara-hafu*, Chinese gable on eaved roof.
貫   *Nuki*, tie.
濡縁   *Nure-en*, "wet veranda," without rain-doors.
塗   *Nuri*, lacquer.

大引   *O-biki*, sleeper joist.
尾極   *Ō-daruki*, projecting rafter-end.
扇極   *Ōgi-daruki*, fan rafters.
鬼瓦   *Oni-gawara*, devil-face tile.
鬼板   *Oni-ita*, devil-face finial.
大奥   *Ō-ōku*, great interior.
折上天井   *Ori-age tenjo*, coved ceiling.
押板   *Oshi-ita*, movable *toko-no-ma*.

欄間   *Ramma*, open-work frieze.
欄干   *Rankan*, balustrade (of important building).
櫺子   *Renji*, lattice window.
車輪藏   *Rinzo*, revolving sutra library.
爐   *Rō*, hearth.
露盤   *Rōban*, nectar pot on summit of roof.
廊下   *Rōka*, corridor.
六角堂   *Rokkakudo*, hexagonal hall.
廊船樓   *Rōsenrō*, covered corridor bridge.
龍舍   *Ryusha*, lower bulb on pagoda pinnacle, "dragon's lair."

三門　　　*Sammon*, two-storied temple gate.
楼唐戸　　*San-karado*, panelled Chinese door.
竿縁天井　*Saobuchi tenjo*, raftered ceiling.
皿斗　　　*Sarato*, echinus of capital.
指肘木　　*Sashi-hijiki*, elbow mortised through pillar.
猿頬天井　*Sarubō-tenjo*, ceiling with bevelled beams.
里内裏　　*Sato dairi*, rural palace.
鞘間　　　*Saya-no-ma*, passage room. Irikawa.
正門　　　*Seimon*, front gate.
銭湯　　　*Sento*, public bath house.
雪隠　　　*Setsuin*, privy (classical).
舎利殿　　*Shariden*, relic hall.
鴟尾　　　*Shibi*, kite-tail roof finials.
澁　　　　*Shibu*, persimmon juice varnish.
七堂伽藍　*Shichido garan*, seven hall monastery.
重棰　　　*Shige-daruki*, double-tiered rafters.
漆喰　　　*Shikkui*, plaster.
錣葺　　　*Shikoro-buki*, gable roof with eaves all round, "helmet curtain roof."
寝殿　　　*Shinden*, palace style residence.
支輪　　　*Shirin*, cove of ceiling or soffit.
下塗　　　*Shita-nuri*, under coat of plaster.
蔀戸　　　*Shitomi*, hanging lattice window.
褥　　　　*Shitone*, sleeping quilt.
書院　　　*Shōin*, study, military mansion style residence.
障子　　　*Shōji*, papered sliding doors.
鐘楼　　　*Shōrō*, belfry.
總門　　　*Sōmon*, front gate of temple.
相輪　　　*Sōrin*, spire of a pagoda.
層輪塔　　*Sōrintō*, pillar-shaped stupa.
縋破風　　*Sugaru hafu*, lean-to gable.
水煙　　　*Suien*, spray-like open-work ornament of spire.
簀　　　　*Sunoko*, bamboo veranda, or seat.
須彌壇　　*Sumidan* (or shumidan), Buddhist altar.

手挟　　　*Tabasami*, rafter strut.
對屋　　　*Tai-no-ya*, wing of Shinden mansion.
匠　　　　*Takumi*, craftsman, carpenter.
溜　　　　*Tamari*, ante-room.

多門   *Tamon*, long building on castle rampart.

棚   *Tana*, shelf, shop.

榱   *Taruki*, rafter.

疊   *Tatami*, floor mat.

疊緣   *Tatami-heri*, floor mat edging.

疊表   *Tatami-omote*, floor mat surface.

亭   *Tei*, pavilion.

天二樣   *Tenjikuyō*, Indian style.

天主閣   *Tenshu-kaku*, castle keep.

手摺   *Tesuri*, railing.

飛梁   *Tobi-bari*, bearer beam, transtrum.

戶袋   *Tō-bukuro*, shutter box.

床柱   *Toko-bashira*, pillar of *tokonoma*.

床の間   *Tokonoma*, alcove for pictures.

料栱   *Tōkyo*, bracket capital.

斗栱   *Tomasu*, measure-shaped capital.

鳥居   *Torii*, shrine portal.

棟梁   *Tōryo*, master carpenter.

東司   *Tōsu*, privies, of a monastery.

遠侍   *Tōzamurai*, outer retainers' chamber.

局   *Tsubone*, court lady's chamber.

衝立   *Tsuitate*, single leaf screen.

附書院   *Tsuke shōin*, projecting window by a *tokonoma*.

妻戶   *Tsumado*, double swing doors.

詰組   *Tsume-gumi*, clustering brackets.

繫虹梁   *Tsunagi-kōryo*, curved collar beam.

釣殿   *Tsuri dono*, fishing pavilion.

釣木   *Tsurugi*, suspender beam.

繧繝間   *Ungen*, shading colours.

鵠の毛通し   *U-no-ke tōshi*, middle verge board of a gable.

上塗   *Uwa-nuri*, upper coat of plaster.

藁葺   *Warabuki*, straw thatch.

藁座   *Waraza*, socket for pivot-hung door.

渡殿   *Wata dono*, covered way.

渡廊   *Watari-rō*, covered corridor.

和樣   *Wayō*, Japanese style.

櫓	*Yagura*, tower.
屋形	*Yakata*, mansion (nobleman).
遣戸	*Yarido*, sliding doors.
屋敷	*Yashiki*, residence of Samurai or Daimyo.
浴室	*Yoku-shitsu*, bathroom.
四足門	*Yotsu-ashi mon*, four-pillared gate.
湯殿	*Yu-dono*, bathroom.
遊廓	*Yūkaku*, pleasure quarter.
湯屋	*Yuya*, public bath house.
座蒲團	*Zabuton*, kneeling cushion.
柘榴口.	*Zakuro-guchi*, bath canopy.
座敷	*Zashiki*, reception room.
禪堂	*Zendo*, meditation hall.
厨子	*Zushi*, small shrine.

BIBLIOGRAPHY

BIBLIOGRAPHY

JAPANESE WORKS

Amanuma Shunichi, Professor, *Nippon Kenchikushi Zuroku* (Illustrations of Japanese Architecture). 6 vols. Kyoto, 1934.

Amanuma Shunichi, Professor, *Nippon Kenchikushi-yo* (Essentials of Japanese Architecture). 2 vols. Tokyo, 1928.

Amanuma Shunichi and Fujiwara Giichi, *Kyoto Bijutsu Taikan Kenchiku* (Survey of the Fine Art of Kyoto—Architecture). Tokyo, 1933.

Architectural Photograph Society, *Kenchiku Shashin Ruiju,* Collection of Architectural Photographs; volumes on Gates, Ceilings, Fences, *Shōji* and *Fusuma,* Garden Gates and Garden Houses, Shrines and Temples etc. Tokyo, 1915.

Bukkyo Bijutsu (Journal of Buddhist Art). Nara, 1924.

Fujii Kōji, Professor, *Nippon no Jutaku* (The Japanese Residence). Tokyo, 1928.

Fujita Motoharu, *Nippon Minka-shi* (History of the Japanese Dwelling House). Tokyo, 1928.

Fujiwara Kinsato, Jukaisho (An Historical Miscellany, *c.* 1460). Tokyo, 1906.

Fukui Yoshinaga, *Wafu Kenchiku Zōzō* (The Construction of Japanese Buildings). Tokyo, 1929.

Hattori Shokichi, *Nippon Ko Kenchikushi* (History of Ancient Japanese Architecture). Kyoto, 1926.

Hiraide Kojiro, *Nippon Fuzokushi* (History of Japanese Customs). Tokyo, 1896.

Ikeda Chujiro, *Daiku-jutsu* (The Art of the Carpenter). Tokyo, 1928.

Imperial Government Railway Department, *O Tera Mairi* (Temples to be Visited). Tokyo, 1922.

Imperial Government Railway Department, *Kami Mode* (Shrines to be Visited). Tokyo, 1933.

Ishizaka Zenjiro, *Ikeda Mitsumasa-kō Den* (Life of Ikeda Mitsumasa, Feudal Lord of Bizen). Tokyo, 1932.

Japanese Academy, *Ruiju Kinsei Fuzokushi* (History of Customs of Recent Times). Tokyo, 1908 (first edition, 1854).

Kaga Shōun-kō (Life of Maeda Tsunatoshi, Feudal Lord of Kaga).

Kenchiku Zasshi (Journal of the Institute of Japanese Architects).

Kōji Ruien, *Jukyobu* (A Catena of Ancient Matters, volume on Residences). Tokyo, 1912.

Kaneko Kentaro, Viscount, *Kuroda Jōsuiden* (Life of Kuroda Jōsui, Feudal Lord of Chikuzen). Tokyo, 1915.

Masuyama Shimpei *Nippon Kenchiku Jidai Yoshiki Kanshiki Zushu* (Illustrated Review of Periods and Styles of Japanese Architecture). Tokyo, 1926.

Mitsuhashi Shiro, *Riso no Kaoku* (The Ideal Residence). 2 vols. Tokyo, 1912.

Nakazawa H. and Others, *Kinai Kembutsu,* (Sights round Kyoto). Tokyo, 1911.

Nippon Rekishi Chiri Gakkai (Japanese Historical and Geographical Society), *Azuchi Jidai Shiron* (Historical Essays on the Asuchi Period). Tokyo, 1915.

Nippon Rekishi Chiri Gakkai, *Edo Jidai Shiron* (Historical Essays on the Edo Period). Tokyo, 1915.

Ono Hitoshi, *Kinsei Jōka Machi no Kenkyu* (Studies of the Castle Town of Recent Times). Tokyo, 1928.

Orui Shin and Toba Masao, *Nippon Jōkakushi* (History of Japanese Castles). Tokyo, 1937.

Saito Kamekichi, *Toko Tana Shōin* (Alcoves, Shelves and Shōin). Tokyo, 1926.

Sato Tasukeru (revised by Professor Amanuma), *Nippon Kenchikushi* (History of Japanese Architecture). Tokyo, 1926.

Takahashi Tatsuo, *Matsudaira Fumai Den* (Life of Matsudaira Fumai, Feudal Lord of Bizen). Tokyo, 1917.

Tanaka Manitsu, *Unjo Hitsuroku* (Mysteries above the Clouds. An Account of the Imperial Court). Tokyo, 1916.

Tayama K. and Nakazawa H., *Onsen Shuyu,* (A Tour of Our Hot Springs). Tokyo, 1922.

Toba Masao, *Edo Jo no Ima Mukashi* (Edo Castle as it Was and Is). Tokyo, 1928.

WORKS IN EUROPEAN LANGUAGES

Cram, Ralph Adams, *Impressions of Japanese Architecture*; the first edition of 1905 reprinted without alteration.

    The first book in English on Japanese architecture as a whole, including sculpture. Its style makes it very pleasant to read; but had it been revised no doubt some things in it would have been altered.

Hideto Kishida, Professor, *Japanese Architecture.* Tourist Library, Japanese Government Railways, Tokyo, 1935.

    An excellent concise and comprehensive introductory survey of the subject written, as are all the volumes of this series, by an eminent authority.

Japan Times and Mail, Architectural Japan, Old and New, by various architectural experts; 1936.

    Dealing with all aspects of architecture and building right up to the present day. Profusely illustrated with fine photographs and plans of every kind of structure, from the temples and tea-rooms of former days to the many blends of traditional and modern functional forms evolved to meet the needs of the commercial, educational, entertainment and religious habits that the post-Meiji age has developed. Town-planning and earthquake damage are included also.

Jiro Harada, *A Glimpse of Japanese Ideals,* 1937.

    Lectures on Japanese Art and Culture. Chapters on Architecture, the Shōsōin, Gardens, Archaeology, Crafts etc. Finely illustrated.

Jiro Harada, *The Lesson of Japanese Architecture.* London, 1937.

> Dr Harada's books are very well written and beautifully illustrated and it would be quite impertinent to criticize them. In this and also in his earlier work (the *Studio* spring number for 1918 on Japanese Gardens) he explains his subject very clearly and shows how the house and garden form a complete framed composition.

Morse, Professor, E.S., *Japanese Homes and their Surroundings.* London, 1888.

> The pioneer work in English on the subject, and even now the best—though long out of print. The author, who was Professor of Zoology in Tokyo, has also written two other works of great interest, *Japan Day by Day*, recently reprinted, and *Glimpses of China and Chinese Homes*, both illustrated by the author's pleasing black-and-white sketches.

Noritake Tsuda, *A Handbook of Japanese Art.* Tokyo, 1936.

> Has many good photographs of the exteriors of famous buildings as well as of their interior decoration, with critical discussions. This is, on the whole, the best and handiest book on Japanese art and craft.

Seiichi Taki, Professor, *Japanese Fine Art.* Tokyo, 1931.

> Has a section on "The Characteristics of Japanese Architecture" which gives a very good summary in its sixty-odd pages.

Taut, Bruno, *Houses and People of Japan.* Sanseido, Tokyo, 1937.

> A book of the same type as that of Morse, but not, I think, so good; for the author, though a professional architect, has not the same experience and knowledge of the country. But his insight and appreciation make it one of the books worth reading.

Tetsuro Yoshida, *Das Japanisches Wohnhaus.* Tokyo, 1936.

> This is quite a masterly and authoritative description of the dwelling house, illustrated by fine photographs and plans, admirable for those who read German, but also useful for those who don't, for the illustrations have much to say.

Tsuyoshi Tamura, Dr, *Art of the Landscape Garden in Japan.*

> Another work that is indispensable to those who would understand the garden setting of the house, which can hardly be illustrated without giving most instructive views of the latter. The same may be said of the book on Japanese Gardens corresponding to that on Architecture in the Tourist Series, by Professor Matsunosuke Tatsui.

INDEX

INDEX

Ajanta, 17, 41
Amado, 52, 59
Ama-no-Kaguyama, 19
Amanuma, *Professor (A Pictorial Record of the History of Japanese Architecture)*, 7, 16, 23, 28, 45, 48, 49, 56, 77
Amida Hall, 33, 38
Amravati Dagoba, 28
Angels, Buddhist, 21
Anrakuji temple, 48
Architects, 99-103
Arima, 55
Ashikaga, period, 4, 7, 93; Shoguns, 47, 91
Ashikaga Yoshiaki, 64
Ashikaga Yoshimasa, 50, 51
Ashikaga Yoshimitsu, 48, 51
Ashikaga Yoshinori, 51, 85
Asoka pillars, 28
Asuka period, 15-19, 21
Azekura style, 24
Azuchi castle, 55, 63, 64

Babylonia, 6
Barbican, 65
Bathrooms, 49, 61, 72, 73, 84, 95
Baths, public, 68, 80, 81
Biwa, Lake, 30
Bō, 26, 30
Bodhisattvas, 34, 38
Bokashi shading, 38
Brackets, 17, 40, 56
Buddhism, introduction of, 11, 15
Burakuin, 31
Butsuden, 40
Byōdōin temple, 35

Castles, 2, 61-6
Ceilings, 91-2
Chanoyu, 50, 59, 61, 78
Chang An, 26
Chidori gable, 58
Chigaidana, 50, 52, 53
Chimaki, pillars, 40
China, influence from, 6, 7, 9, 13-19, 27, 39
Chō, 26, 30

Chōdai, 10
Chōdōin, 26, 31
Chorten, 18
Chou Li, 11, 13
Chudan, 11
Chūmon, 18
Churches, Christian, 7, 55
Chusonji, 36-7
Colleges, Christian, 55; Confucian, 79
Confucius, 13; analects of, 98
Constantinople, 70
Crane Chamber, 60

Daibenjo, 93
Daianji temple, 99
Dai-dempōin, 47
Daigōji, 38
Daigo Sambōin, 57
Daikyoku Bashira, 10
Daikyoku Den, 19, 26, 31
Daimyos, 53, 65, 68, 70, 75, 77, 79, 81; mansions of, 82, 83
Dais Chamber, 59, 60, 61, 72
Dairi, 30
Daito, 18, 28
Daitokuji temple, 40, 58, 102
Daruma, 53
Daulatabad, 70
Dempōdō (Hōryuji), 24
Dengyo Daishi, 27, 28, 32
Denka, 3
Dōgō, 95
Dōji, monk, 99
Doric order, 16

Ebi kōryō, 41
Echizen, province, 10, 13
Eckardt, A. (*Korean Art*), 17
Edo castle, 2, 69-74
Edo period, 6, 16, 55, 67-84; kitchens of, 98
Eight-roofed style, 58
Eihōji, Kaisando, 42, 58, 74
Eirokuji, 55
Engakuji, Shariden, 41
Engawa, 12
Enryakuji (Hieizan), 28
Eunuchs, 74

Ferguson, J., 2
Firearms, introduction of, 62
Frog-crotches, 17, 66
Führer-Heimendorf, von H. (*Naked Nagas*), 8
Fujita, *Professor*, 7, 14
Fujiwara Fuhito, 21
Fujiwara Hidehira, 37
Fujiwara Kiyohira, 37
Fujiwara Michinaga, 35, 36
Fujiwara Motohira, 37
Fujiwara period, 27, 33-9; palace of, 19; regents of, 27, 33, 34, 35
Fujiwara Sadaie, 36
Fijiwara Yorimichi, 35
Fukiage park, 71
Fukiji temple, 38
Funa hijiki, 17
Fushimi Inari shrine, 37
Fushimi Momoyama castle, 55
Fusuma, 52, 80, 90

Gandhara, 6, 19
Gankōji, 22-3
Garan, 17
Gardens, 5, 103
Gates, 3, 40, 81, 82
Gedan, 11
Gembo, monk, 99
Gemmyo, *Empress*, 22
Genji, *Prince*, 35, 36
Genroku era, 72
Ginkaku, 50, 63
Gion shrine, 37
Gishōji temple, 50
Go Daigo, *Emperor*, 45
Goemon-buro, 95
Go Fukakusa, *Emperor*, 45
Go Hanazono, *Emperor*, 85
Go Kameyama, *Emperor*, 45
Gongen style, 38, 42, 58
Gō Roju, 68
Go Saga, *Emperor*, 45
Go Shirakawa, *Emperor*, 33, 44
Great Council of the Shogun, 68
Gupta era, 17

Hachiman shrine, 29
Hakuho period, 20
Hukuzan shrine, 90
Harada, Jiro (*The Lesson of Japanese Architecture*), 50, 59, 83
Hatto (Doctrine Hall), 40
Hatamoto, 70, 83
Havell, E. B. (*Indian Architecture*), 25
Hearth God, 98
Heaven of Brahma, 63
Heian period, 27-38, 80, 90
Heiden (Hall of Offerings), 58
Heijo, capital of, 25
Heika, 3
Heinai family, 67, 78
Hida, province, 13
Hidari Jingoro, 60
Hideyori. *See* Toyotomi
Hideyoshi. *See* Toyotomi
Hi-dono (gutter-chamber), 94
Hieizan, 28, 32
Higashiyama, 37
Hikite, 59
Hikone castle, 65, 83
Himeji castle, 65
Himorogi, 13
Hira-iri, 9
Hirado, 69
Hiroma, 52
Hiroshima castle, 65
Hiunkaku, 57, 59, 60-1, 63
Hiyoshi shrine, 29
Hōjō, 40
Hōjō Tokimune, 41
Hōkōji, 56
Hokkedo (Tōdaiji), 23
Hokkiji, 15, 18
Hokuriku district, 53
Hon-ami Kō-etsu, 57, 102
Hongwanji, Nishi, 59-60; monks of the, 62, 64
Hon maru, 63, 70
Hō-ō-do, 35, 38
Hōryuji, temple, 7, 15, 16, 23, 24; pagoda, 17
Hōtō pagoda, 18
Hyōtoku, 98

Ieyasu. *See* Tokugawa
Iga district, 11
Ikeda Mitsumasa, 11, 80
Ima Monogatari, 95
Imperial Palace, 3, 8, 19, 23, 26, 30, 31, 35, 43, 51, 58, 79
Inari, the Food God, 9
Inns, 83-4
Irikawa, 59, 83
Irimoya, 9, 29, 37, 51

Ise shrine, 8, 9
Ishiyama, 64
Istambul, 74
Ita-buro, 95
Ito, *Professor*, 7
Itsukushima shrine, 45
Izanami and Izanagi, 10
Izumi Dono, 35
Izumo shrine, 9, 10, 13, 14

Jetavana Vihara, 7
Jijuden, 32
Jimmu, *Emperor*, 19
Jingo, *Empress*, 5
Jito, *Empress*, 19
Jizai, 98
Jodan, 11
Jōdō sect, 39
Juraku mansion, 55, 59, 67

Kaeru-mata, 17
Kagoshima castle, 65
Kairyūōji pagoda, 21
Kalasha (nectar pot), 25
Kamakura era, 6, 25, 39, 40-6, 90-1
Kameyama, *Emperor*, 45
Kami Daigo, 43
Kamo shrine, 29
Kaneiji temple, 75, 78
Kangakuin (Enjōji temple), 46
Kanin palace, 35
Kano Eitoku, 60, 61
Kano Sanraku, 61
Kano Tannyu, 60, 72
Kanshin, monk, 99
Kanshinji composite style, 44, 54
Kara style, 39, 42, 47, 49, 54, 58, 66, 78
Kara-hafu, 45
Karakusa (vine scrolls), 19
Kasuga, *Lady*, 74
Kasuga shrine, 29
Kato-mado, 41
Katsura palace, 58
Kawaya, 94
Kennniji, 78, 94
Kenrei-mon, 31
Kesho-yane-ura, 91
Kibitsu shrine, 50
Kida, *Professor*, 7, 12, 26
Kinkakuji, 48, 49, 63
Kita-no-kata, 3, 46
Kitano, Tenjin, 58, 74
Kitchens, 97-8
Kiyomori, Taira, 45, 77
Kiyomizu temple, 29, 78
Kō-no-Moronao, 52
Kōbō Daishi, 27, 28, 32, 33
Kobori Enshu, 59, 102

Kōdō, 16
Kōfukuji temple, 21, 22
Kōgyoku, *Emperor*, 12
Kōgyoku, *Empress*, 19
Kōhōan villa, 102
Kōji, 26
Kōjiki, 8, 14, 94
Kōken, *Empress*, 23
Kōmyo, *Empress*, 24, 25
Kōndo, 15, 22-3
Kongobuji temple, 28
Kōnin era, 27, 28
Kora family, 72, 75, 102
Korea, 6, 15, 17
Kōryo, 18
Kōshin, 98
Kōya, Mount, 28, 32, 94
Kudara, 15, 16
Kumamoto castle, 65
Kumo-hijiki, 17
Kunōzan, 74
Kura, 80
Kuroki-no-miya, 19
Kuro Shōin, 73, 74
Kuruwa, 63
Kyōgoku, 26, 30
Kyoto, 12, 29

Leach, Bernard (*A Potter's Book*), 100
Liang, Southern, 15
Liang Chou Lai Tien, 14
Li Ki, 98
Lloyd, Nathaniel (*History of the English House*), 6
Lucas, E. V., 5

Maeda, *Lord*, 82
Mairado, 50, 59, 91
Maitreyya, 33
Mampukuji temple, 78
Manyōshu, 13, 19
Maru, 63
Masugata gate, 65
Matsudaira Fumai, 102
Matsudaira Sadanobu, 31, 79
Matsunaga Hisahide, 42
Mausolea, Imperial, 75, 103
Meiji era, 7, 20
Mi-Daidokoro, 3, 73
Mikado, 3
Mikumari shrine, 45
Ming dynasty, 78
Mitsuhashi (*Riso no Kaoku*), 72
Miyajima, 45, 77
Miyako, capital of Heian, 29
Mizuya, 97
Momiji-yama, 75
Mommu, *Emperor*, 19, 22
Momoyama period, 54-66
Mon-in, 3

Index

Monto Amida sect, 55
Mori, 12, 13
Mori, Motonari, *Lord*, 45
Murakami, *Emperor*, 35
Murasaki, *Lady*, 36
Murōji, 25, 29
Muromachi period, 47-53
Myōshinji refectory, 57, 79

Naga-tsubone, 72
Nagasaki, 55, 78
Nagoya castle, 65
Naka-oku, 71
Nambanji, 55 ·
Nandaimon, 16, 18, 42
Nando, 10, 12
Nankyo, 29
Nanzenji temple, 40, 78
Nara, period, 14, 20, 21-6;
  the capital at, 25-6, 29, 30
Nichiren sect, 39, 55
Nihongi, 8
Nihon Shoki, 11
Nijo castle, 71, 73
Nikko Toshogu, 58, 67, 74
Ni-no-maru, 63, 70
Nishi-maru, 71
Nobunaga. *See* Oda
North and South Dynasties,
  16
No-tenjo ceiling, 57

Obaku sect, 78
Oda Nobunaga, 63-4
Ogimachi, *Emperor*, 58
O-heisoku, 41
Oji, 26
O-kawa, 94
Okayama, castle, 64, 65, 83;
  province, 98
Omoto, 57
Onamuji, 94
Ōnin period, 47, 51
Ō-oku, 71, 73
Ō-omote, 71
Osaka castle, 63-4
Otomo, Daimyo, 53
Otori shrine, 10, 11
O Yue, 10

Pagoda, 17; octagonal, 48
Palace, Imperial. *See* Im-
  perial Palace
Parthenon, 19
Peking, 70, 74
Persia, 6, 24
Pillars, Azoka, 28; centre,
  10; *chimaki*, 40; of Azuka
  period, 16-17, 18
Polynesian houses, 14
Portuguese, influence of, 62,
  64

Privy, 93-5

Rafters, dressed open, 91
Ramma, 46, 52, 59
Rasho-mon, 30
Rats, 91-2
Restaurants, 68, 84, 91, 93
Rishi, Taoist, 64
Roofs, boarded, 53
Ryobu Shinto, 32
Ryūkoin temple, 28

Sages, Confucian, 64
Saikyo, 29
Saimei, *Empress*, 19
Saionji Kintsune, 48
Sakai Tadakatsu, 77, 78
Sammon gate, 40
Samurai, 46, 52, 53, 62, 68,
  81, 83
Sanchi, 17
Sanetomo, Minamoto, 41
Sanjusangendo, Kyoto, 37,
  44
San-no-maru, 65, 70
Saobuchi-tenjo, 91
Saruho-tenjo, 91
Sashi-hijiki, 41, 51
Sato Dairi, 35, 45
Scott, Gilbert, 16
Sei Shonagon, *Lady*, 36
Seido, 79
Seiryōden, 32, 58, 95
Seiyōsho, 94
Sekino, *Professor*, 7, 16, 26
Sento, 81
Senyōden, 51, 58
Sen Rikyu, 61
Setsuin, 94
Shiba, 75
Shiba Tachito, 15
Shibi, 17
Shichido Garan, 16, 20
Shigehira, Taira, 39
Shimazu, house of, 62
Shimmei style, 29
Shin sect, 39
Shinden residence, 34, 53, 57
Shingon Buddhism, 27, 28
Shin Yakushiji temple, 23
Shirakawa, 13
Shiro Shōin, 73, 74
Shishinden, 12, 31, 34, 58, 79
Shitennōji, 16, 18
Shitomi, 36, 46, 52, 90
Shizuoka, 74
Shōgi, 12
Shōin style, 46, 51-3, 57, 59,
  73
Shōji, 6, 11, 35, 52, 90;
  waist-high, 50, 60, 90
Shokenden, 60

Shoku Sanjin, 92
Shops, 83
Shombenjo, 93
Shōmu, *Emperor*, 23
Shōsōin (storehouse), 23
Shōtoku, *Prince*, 18, 24
Shugaku, palace, 79; high-
  way, 19, 26, 30
Shunjōbō Jōgen, 42
Si Wang Mu, 60
Six Dynasties, 14
Soga-no-Iname, 15
Soga-no-Umako, 15
Sōrin, 21, 48
Sōrinto, 28
South and North Dynasties,
  16
Stambha, 28
Stone chamber, 58, 78
Stoves, 98
Strzygowski, *Professor*, J.
  (*Early Church Art in
  Northern Europe*), 2
Stupa, 17, 28
Sui dynasty, 20
Suiko, *Empress*, 15, 17, 45
Suinin, *Emperor*, 8, 14
Sujin, *Emperor*, 13
Sumiyoshi shrine, 10
Susa-no-O, 13
Sutoku, *Emperor*, 35
Sung dynasty, 41
Swastika, 17

Tabasami, 44, 66
Tachibana, *Lady*, 25
Tahōtō pagoda, 21
Taika (Great Reform), 20
Taikenmonin, *Empress*, 35
Taira Kiyomori, 45
Taira Shigehira, 39
Taiyuin shrine, 78
Takagamine, 102
Takeda Shingen, 62, 94-5
Tamura, *Dr* (*Landscape
  Gardens*), 50
Tamamushi shrine, 17
T'ang dynasty, 20, 22, 26, 27,
  33, 39, 60, 61
Tatami, 5, 11, 46, 52
Tat'ung caves, 17
Tea Masters, 67
Tea-rooms, 50, 57, 91
Teishakuten (Heaven of
  Brahma), 63
Tempyo period, 21, 22
Temples, dimensions of, 87,
  88; Greek, 13; Zen, 40-1,
  51, 52, 78, 79
Tenchi, *Emperor*, 19
Tendai Buddhism, 27, 28

Index

Tenjiku style, 39, 41, 42, 54, 56, 57, 78
Tenjin shrine, Kitano, 58, 74
Tenjo, 91
Tenshu, 63
Theatres, 68, 70
Titles deriving from architecture, 3
Tōdaiji, 22, 23, 39, 42, 43, 56, 78
Tōfukuji, 41
Tōji, 29, 57
Tokonoma, 52, 53
Tokugawa Hidetada, 67, 71, 75, 79
Tokugawa Iemitsu, 58, 67, 70, 71, 74, 75, 78, 87
Tokugawa Ienari, 79
Tokugawa Ietsuna, 67, 80
Tokugawa Ieyasu, 38, 56, 58, 65, 67, 68, 69, 70, 71, 74, 75
Tokugawa Tsunayoshi, 67, 73, 79
Tokugawa Yoshimune, 88
Tokutomi Sōhō, 63
Tokyudo, 50
Tono, 3
Tonomo, 46, 59, 60

Toshōdaiji temple, 22, 23, 38
Tōsu, 40, 94
Tout, B., 78
Toyokuni shrine, 56, 67
Toyotomi Hideyoshi, 7, 47, 54, 55-8, 63, 64, 68, 95
Toyotomi Hideyori, 56, 63
Tozamurai, 46, 52
Tsubone, 3, 73
Tsuda, *Dr (Handbook of Japanese Art)*, 34
Tsuji-ban, 81
Tsuma-iri, 9
Tsume-gumi, 40
Tsuri Dono, 35

Uchi-samurai, 46
Uda, *Emperor*, 27
Ueno, 75
Ukita, 64
Unebi, Mount, 19
University, Imperial, 30, 82

Vases, Greek, 19

Wa style, 39, 54, 57, 58
Wakamatsu castle, 68
Wei, North, 17

Wu Sung 27
Wu, *Emperor*, 60

Yagura, 46
Yakushiji, pagoda, 21; temple, 22, 38
Yashiki, 69
Yellow Crane Terrace, 61
Yodo River, 30
Yōmei gate, 76
Yoritomo, Minamoto, 39
Yoshida, T. (*Das Japonishes Wohnhaus*), 50, 59
Yoshimasa, Yoshimitsu, Yoshinori, Yoshiaki. *See* Ashikaga
Yugito, 28, 75
Yume-dono (Hōryuji), 16, 23, 24
Yūryaku, *Emperor*, 14
Yuzu Nembutsu sect, 39

Zen sect, 39, 40, 41, 51, 52, 78, 79, 99
Zendo, 40
Zenkōji, 12
Zōzōji, 75

PLATES

Plate 1

Plate 1

FIG. 1

FIG. 2

FIG. 3

Forms of ancient houses. FIGS 1 and 3. Clay models from dolmens.
FIG. 2. Engravings on mirrors.

Plate 2

FIG. 1. FIG. 2. FIG. 3. FIG. 4. FIG. 5. FIG. 6.

FIG. 1. Plan of Izumo shrine.   FIG. 2. Plan of Otori shrine.   FIG. 3. Plan of Sumiyoshi shrine.   FIG. 4. Umbrella shape plan of early house.   1. Front room.   2. Kitchen.   3, 4. Living-rooms.   FIG. 5. Conjectured most ancient form of house called Tenchi Kongen Miya-zukuri. FIG. 6. The Great Shrine of Izumo, rebuilt in 1744, Edo period.   Front view, plan and side view.

Plate 3

FIG. 1

FIG. 2

FIG. 1. The Ise Daijingu or Main Shrine at Ise. Unique Shimmei style. Front and side views. FIG. 2. Ordinary Shimmei style shrine. Front and side views.

Plate 4

The Sumiyoshi shrine.   Rebuilt in 1709.   Edo period.   Front view, plan and side view.

Plate 5

FIG. 1.

FIG. 2.

FIG. 3.

FIG. 1. Kokuchu Sumai house in Iga district of Shiga prefecture. (*a*) Entrance. (*b*) Earth-floored kitchen. (*c*) Threshold beam (*Fuki*). (*d*) Sitting-room with floor covered with bran 2 inches deep and laid with straw matting, called *nyuji*. (*e*) Inner room with boarded floor for master and mistress. (*f*) Sleeping room, board floor. (*g*) Buddhist shrine. (*h*) Cupboard, (*i*) Kitchen stove. (*j*) Kitchen sink. (*k*) Bathroom. (*l*) Pissoir. (*m*) Disused stable. (*x*) *Tokonoma*.

FIG. 2. Old house in Amatsu village, Tansei district, Echizen province. (*a*) Buddhist shrine. (*b*) *Tokonoma*. (*c*) Great centre pillar (*daikyoku*). (*d*) Hearth. (*e*) Quilt warmer (*kotatsu*). (*f*) Bathroom. (*g*) Entrance. (*h*) Privy. (*i*) Oi-no-kami (upper house). (*j*) Oi-no-shimo (lower house).

FIG. 3. (*a*) House at Shirakawa, Hida province, with plan of lower story. There are four stories but the upper two are only used for storing fodder. Length, 54 feet; depth, 44 feet. (*a*) Entrance passage. (*b*) Living-room. (*c*) Reception room. (*d*) Inner room. (*e*) Chamber. (*f*) Buddhist shrine chamber. (*g*) Chamber. (*h*) Kitchen. (*i*) Bath. (*j*) Sink. (*k*) Hearth. (*l*) Rice-pounding place. (*m*) Stable. (*n*) Veranda.

Plate 6

FIG. 1

FIG. 2

FIG. 1. House in Tansei village, Iga district of Shiga prefecture, showing north, south, east and west aspects. An example of the Kokuchu Sumai type, like the Otori shrine, with two pillars instead of the one of the Iga style. (*a*) Entrance. (*b*) Earth-floored space. (*c*) Raised beam. (*d*) Daikoku pillar. (*e*) Shokaku pillar. (*f*) Kitchen. (*g*) Nyuji. (*h*) Sitting-room. (*i*) Chamber. (*j*) Buddhist shrine. (*k*) Tokonoma. (*l*) Bathroom. (*m*) Privy. (*n*) Utensil cupboard. (*o*) Shelf. (*p*) Hearth.

FIG. 2. Old house in Iwakura village, Otagi district, Kyoto prefecture. (*a*) Entrance. (*b*) Earth-floored kitchen. (*c*) Wooden dining bench (*shōgi*). (*d*) Shelf. (*e*) Sink. (*f*) Step up. (*g*) Oue. (*h*) Nando. (*i*) Sitting-room. (*j*) Inner sitting-room. (*k*) *Tokonoma*. (*l*) Buddhist shrine. (*m*) Cupboards. (*n*) Stable. (*o*) Kitchen stove.

Plate 7

Sites of the ancient capitals in Yamato.

Plate 8

The capital of Asuka. Imperial mausolea.

Plate 9

Pillars. Fig. 1. Kōnin era, 810-824. Early Heian period. Murōji pagoda. Fig. 2. Tempyo era, 729-749. Late Nara period. Eisanji Hakkakudo Toshodaiji. Kondo. Fig. 3. Haku-ho era, 673-686. Early Nara period. Yakushiji pagoda. Fig. 4. Asuka or Suiko era, 590-630. Hōryuji, Kondo. Hōryuji, Kondo, Chūmon.

Fig. 1. Fig. 2. Fig. 3. Fig. 4.

Plate 10

Pillars. Fig. 1. Kamakura period, 1185-1392. Kawachi, Kanshinji (Kanshinji style). Tōdaiji, Hokkedo (Japanese new style), Wayo Shimpa. Fig. 2. Harima, Jodoji (Indian style), Tenjikuoy. Fig. 3. Engakuji (T'ang style), Karayo. Fig. 4. Fujiwara period, 824-1185. Byodoin Ho-odo Rikuchu. Chusonji.

Plate 11

Pillars. Fig. 1. Edo period, 1600-1868. Nikko Taiyuin. Fig. 2. Momoyama period, 1568-1600. Kyoto, Daitokuji. Kyoto, Toyokuni shrine. Kyoto, Toyokuni shrine. Fig. 3. Muromachi period, 1392-1568. Kyoto, Kinkakuji. Kyoto, Tōfukuji. Mino, Eihōji.

Plate 12

FIG. 1

FIG. 2

FIG. 3

Elbow brackets. FIG. 1. Single bracket. FIG. 2. Double bracket. FIG. 3. Triple bracket.

Plate 13

FIG. 1.   FIG. 2.   FIG. 3.   FIG. 4.   FIG. 5.

FIG. 1. Sextuple brackets.   FIG. 2. Quintuple brackets.   FIG. 3. Septuple brackets.
FIG. 4. Groups of three (*koshi-gumi*).   FIG. 5. Close grouping (*tsume-gumi*).

Plate 14

FIG. 1. Frog-crotches of the Asuka and Heian eras. 1 and 2, Hōryuji. 3 and 4, Toshōdaiji. 5, Uji shrine. 6 and 7, Chusonji. 8, Kami-Daigo Yakushiji. 9, Hōōdo.

FIG. 2. Frog-crotches of the Muromachi and Momoyama periods. 1, Ninomiya shrine, Kawachi. 2, Toyokuni shrine gate, Kyoto. 3, Chikurinji shrine, Tosa. 4, Toji temple, Kyoto. 5, Sugino village shrine, Chiga.

Plate 15

FIG. 1

FIG. 2

FIG. 3

FIG. 4

FIG. 5

FIG. 1. Tail-rafter bracket-supports (*tabasami*), Kamakura period. FIGS 2-5. King-post construction of Kamakura and later periods. FIG. 2. Tōdaiji Hokkedo. FIG. 3. Tamahiko shrine. FIG. 4. Kokuseiji Kanshodo. FIG. 5. Kitano shrine.

*Plate 15*A

Fig. 1. Relic casket in the shape of a tope from Manikyala, first century A.D. Fig. 2. Bracket capital of the fifth century at Nassick. Fig. 3. Pillar and capital of the fifth century at Ajanta. Fig. 4. Lotus and water pot capital of India. Fig. 5. Palace facade at Barhut showing pipal leaf window arches. Fig. 6. Bracket and strut construction of eleventh century at Mount Abu. Fig. 7. Nepalese Dagoba. Fig. 8. Wooden Jaina temple at Canara.

Plate 16

Fig. 1

Fig. 2

FIG. 1. Professor Amanuma's restoration of the Kondo of the Hōryuji.   FIG. 2. Section of
the cloister gallery of the Hōryuji.

Plate 17

The Kondo of the Hōryuji, elevation and section.

Plate 18

The five-storied pagoda of the Hōryuji.

Plate 19

Elbow brackets of the earliest period. Hōryuji temple, seventh century.

Plate 20

FIG. 1. Kudara style, Hōryuji type.   FIG. 2. Kudara style, Shitennōji type.   FIG. 3. Kara
style (Nara), T'ang.   FIG. 4. Zen style (Kamakura), Sung.

Plate 21

The capital of Heijo at Nara.

Plate 22

Plate 23

FIG. 1

FIG. 2

FIG. 3

FIG. 4

FIGS 1 and 2. Three-branch bracketing of the pagoda of the Yakushiji. FIG. 3. Pierced iron "spray" (*suien*) of the pinnacle of the Yakushiji pagoda. FIG. 4. Large and small capitals of the bracketing of the above.

Plate 24

FIG. 1

FIG. 2

FIG. 1. Plan of the Hōryuji temple. M 1. Nandai-mon (south gate). F 2. Jotomon. K 3. Shindo. A 4. Chumon (middle gate). A 5. Cloister. A 6. Kondo (Golden hall). A 7. Pagoda. F 8. Bell-tower. K 9. Library. F 10. Lecture hall. K 11. Upper hall. K 12. Jizo hall. K 13. Yakushi hall. K 14. Sankyoin. M 15. Bath house. 16 Goma hall. K 17. Seireiin. K 18. Tsuma-shitsu. K 19. Storehouse. T 20. Refectory. K 21. Loggia. M 22. Todaimon (east gate). T 23. Ritsugakuin. T 24. Yume-dono. M 25. Cloister. M 26. Nandaimon. K 27. Reido. K 28. Shariden. T 29. Dempodo. K 30. Bell-tower.

[A, Asuka (seventh century); T. Tempyo (eighth century); F, Fujiwara (ninth and tenth century); K, Kamakura (thirteenth century); M, Muromachi (fourteenth and fifteenth century).]

FIG. 2. Plan of the Tōdaiji temple as it was in the Tempyo era (729-748). 1. Lecture hall. 2. Library. 3. Belfry. 4. North hall. 5. East hall. 6. West hall. 7. Refectory. 8. North central gate. 9. Great Buddha hall. 10. Cloister. 11. West central gate. 12. East central gate. 13. South central gate. 14. West pagoda. 15. East pagoda. 16. South great gate. 17. Great belfry. 18. Hokke hall. 19. Kensakudo. 20. Kaidanin. 21. West great gate. 22. Middle gate. 23. Sahoji gate. 24. Shōsōin.

Plate 25

FIG. 1. Kondo of the Toshōdaiji. FIG. 2. Section of the Toshōdaiji. FIG. 3. Detail of bracketing of the Toshōdaiji. FIG. 4. Side view of the Toshōdaiji.

Plate 26

FIG. 1

FIG. 2

FIG. 1. Yume-dono of the Hōryuji temple.   FIG. 2. Water-pot pinnacle (*roban*) of the
Yume-dono.

Plate 27

Plate 28

83.

230.8.

8.

FIG. 1

FIG. 2

FIG. 1. Professor Amanuma's restoration of the seven-story pagoda of the Tōdaiji. FIG. 2. Hokkedo of the Tōdaiji.

Plate 29

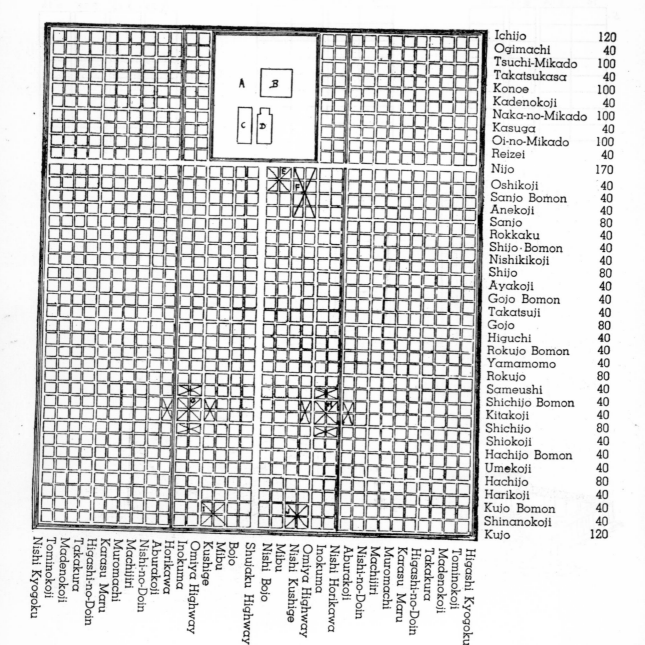

Ichijo — 120
Ogimachi — 40
Tsuchi-Mikado — 100
Takatsukasa — 40
Konoe — 100
Kadenokoji — 40
Naka-no-Mikado — 100
Kasuga — 40
Oi-no-Mikado — 100
Reizei — 40
Nijo — 170

Oshikoji — 40
Sanjo Bomon — 40
Anekoji — 40
Sanjo — 80
Rokkaku — 40
Shijo·Bomon — 40
Nishikikoji — 40
Shijo — 80
Ayakoji — 40
Gojo Bomon — 40
Takatsuji — 40
Gojo — 80
Higuchi — 40
Rokujo Bomon — 40
Yamamomo — 40
Rokujo — 80
Sameushi — 40
Shichijo Bomon — 40
Kitakoji — 40
Shichijo — 80
Shiokoji — 40
Hachijo Bomon — 40
Umekoji — 40
Hachijo — 80
Harikoji — 40
Kujo Bomon — 40
Shinanokoji — 40
Kujo — 120

Nishi Kyogoku — 120
Tominokoji — 40
Madenokoji — 40
Takakura — 40
Higashi-no-Doin — 80
Karasu Maru — 40
Muromachi — 40
Machijiri — 40
Nishi-no-Doin — 80
Aburakoji — 40
Horikawa — 80
Inokuma — 40
Omiya Highway — 120
Kushige — 40
Mibu — 100
Bojo — 40
Shujaku Highway — 280
Nishi Bojo — 40
Mibu — 100
Nishi Kushige — 40
Inokuma — 40
Nishi Horikawa — 120
Omiya Highway — 40
Inokuma — 80
Aburakoji — 40
Nishi-no-Doin — 80
Machijiri — 40
Muromachi — 40
Karasu Maru — 40
Higashi-no-Doin — 80
Takakura — 40
Madenokoji — 40
Tominokoji — 40
Higashi Kyogoku — 120

The Heian Capital (Heian no Miyako).
(A) Imperial City. (B) Palace. (C) Horaku-in. (D) Hasshō-in. (E) University.
(F) Shinsen-en park. (G) Right market. (H) Left market. (I) Saiji. (J) Toji. (Numbers
indicate width of streets in feet.)

Plate 30

FIG. 1

FIG. 2

FIG. 3

FIG. 4

FIG. 5
The Heian Capital

Lay-out of a block (*cho*) of thirty-two rows.   FIG. 1. Block fronting on a wide street.
FIG. 2. Normal inside block.   FIG. 3. Shopping block.   FIG. 4. Lay-out of the eastern
market.   (*a*) Outer blocks.   (*b*) Inner block.   (*c*) Market buildings.   (*d*) Market administration.   (*e*) Schichijo Bomon.   (*f*) Schijo.   (*g*) Omiya.   (*h*) Horikawa.   FIG. 5. The Shishinden or throne hall with the Nan-en or southern court in front of it.   Facing it is the
Shomei gate and on each side are the Nikka-mon and Gekka-mon, the sun and moon gates
on the left and right respectively (looking from the Shishinden).   On the left side also
is the Giyoden hall.   On each side of the entrance of the Shishinden are the cherry-tree of
the left and the orange of the right.

The Heian Capital

The Dai-Dairi or Imperial City with the Palace, the Hasshōin and Hōgakuin halls of ceremony, the eight departments of State and the various palace and government offices. Kōnin period (810-824).

1. *Nuri-shitsu*, lacquer room. 2. *Ogimi-tsukasa*, Princes' bureau. 3. *Uneme-tsukasa*, Court ladies. 4. *Hyogo-ryo*, arsenal. 5. *Okura-sho*, treasury office. 6. *Okura*, treasury. 7. *Naga-dono*. 8. *Ritsubun-kura*, tax storehouse. 9. *Tonomo-ryo*, palace furniture office. 10. *O-tonoi*, night watch. 11. Guard-house. 12. *Cha-en*, tea gardens. 13. *Naikyo-bo*, dancing school. 14. *Ukonei-fu*, right bodyguard. 15. *Uhyoei-fu*, right guards. 16. *Butokuden*, martial exercise hall. 17. *Dzusho-ryo*, library. 18. *O-uta-dokoro*, poetry bureau. 19. *Kamon-ryo*, palace cleaning bureau. 20. *Kura-ryo*, storehouse department. 21. *Nui-ryo*, dress-making department. 22. *Nan-in*. 23. *Nashimoto*, detached palace. 24. *Sakonei-fu*, left bodyguard. 25. *Sahyoei-fu*, left guards. 26. *Toga-in* and 27. *Saiga-in*, Palace of Crown Prince. 28. *Takumi-ryo*, board of works. 29. *Miki-tsukasa*, sake brewery. 30. *Sama-ryo*, left horse guard. 31. *Uma-ryo*, right horse guard. 32. *Tengaku-ryo*. music bureau. 33. Palace well. 34. *Nakatsukasa-sho*, intermediary department. 35. *Jibu-sho*, officials' department. 36. *Sho-ryo*, mausoleum bureau. 37. *Gemba*, foreign affairs. 38. *Hanji*, justiciary. 39. *Gyobu-sho*, justice department. 40. *Danjo-dai*, censors' bureau. 41. *Hyobu-sho*, war office. 42. *Hōgaku-in*. 43. *Hassho-in*. 44. *Shingon-in*, Buddhist chapel. 45. *Ito-dokoro*, weaving office. 46. *Naizen-tsukasa*, Imperial kitchens. 47. *Uneme-machi*, Court ladies. 48. *Moku-ryo*, building bureau. 49. *Chiuwa-in*, hall of worship. 50. *Dairi*, palace. 51. *Geki-dono*, Imperial Edicts. 52. *Nansho*. 53. *Ippon-gosho*. 54. *Kama-dokoro*. 55. *Naiju-dokoro*, pages department. 56. *Shiki-mizoshi*, ministers' bureau. 57. *Inyo-ryo*, astrology department. 58. *Jiju-kyoku*, chamberlains. 59. *Uchi-toneri*, Imperial Attendants. 60. *Kemmotsu*, keeper of the keys. 61. *Shurei*. 62. *Shuitsu*. 63. *Dajokan*, privy council department. 64. *Kageyu*, accountants' bureau. 65. *Mimbu-sho*, home department. 66. *Chikara*, taxation. 67. *Kazue*, revenue. 68. *Shikibu-sho*, ceremonies department. 69. *Sai-in*. 70. *I-in*, physicians' bureau. 71. *Mondo*, water-works bureau. 72. *Daizen-shoku*, culinary office. 73. *Kunai-sho*, Imperial household. 74. *Oi-ryo*, Imperial Cereal Food. 75. *Rin-in*, rice storehouse. 76. *Jingi-kan*, board of religion. 77. *Jiju-cho*, chamberlains' office. 78. *Uta-ryo*, music.

Plate 31

Plate 32

The Heian Capital

Imperial Palace. 1. Kurando lodgings. 2. Department of presents. 3. Vermilion utensil hall.
4. Imperial palanquin house. 5. Flushing hall. 6. Bamboos. 7. Cherry-tree. 8. Orange-tree.
9. Pear-tree (*nashi*). 10. Paullownia (*kiri*). 11. Wistaria-tree (*fuji*). 12. Plum-tree (*ume*).

Plate 33

FIG. 1

FIG. 2

The Heian Capital
FIG. I. The Chōdōin or Hasshōin. 1. Daikyokuden or throne chamber. 2. Shoanden or ante-chamber. FIG. 2. The Hōgakuin.

The Heian Capital

The plan of the Seiryoden of the palace. 1. Front veranda. 2. Seiryoden hall. 3. Earth floor. 4. Bed chamber (Yoru-no-otodo). 5. First consort's chamber (Kokiden-no-ue-no-tsubone). 6. Second consort's chamber (Fujitsubo-no-ue-no-tsubone). 7. Lespedeza chamber (Hagi-no-ma). 8. Ante-chamber. 9. Kitchen (Daibansho). 10. Devil chamber (Oni-no-ma). 11. Dining-room (Asa-garei-no-ma). 12. Lavatory. 13. Dressing-room (On-yudono-agari). 14. Bathroom (On-yudono). 15. North-west corridor. 16. Dining-room court. 17. Middle corridor. 18. Kitchen court. 19. South-west corridor. 20. Reception chamber. 21. Divine fairy gate (Shinsen-mon). 22. Nameless gate (Mumei-mon). 23. Vestibule. 24. Guard-room (Shita-zamurai). 25. Covered porch. 26. Gate of revered benevolence (Sujin-mon). 27. Covered bridge. 28. Archery ground. 29. Archery pavilion. 30. Stream. 31. Bamboo veranda (Sunoko). 30. Recorders (Kurando). 31. Night watch (Tonoi). 32. Ditch.

Plate 34

Plate 35

F<small>IG</small>. 1

F<small>IG</small>. 1. Nobleman's mansion of the Fujiwara age in Shinden style.   F<small>IG</small>. 2. Plan
of Shinden style mansion.   (*a*) Shinden.
(*b*) Tai.   (*c*) Izumi-dono (water pavilion).   (*d*) Tsuri-dono (fishing pavilion).   (*e*)   Gates.   (*f*) Car house.
(*g*)· Island.   (*h*)   Family   apartments.
(*i*) Corridors.

F<small>IG</small>. 2

Plate 36

Fig. 1

Fig. 2

Fig. 1. Plan of the Kanin palace. 1. Shishinden. 2. Jijuden. 3. Seiryoden. 4. Giyōden. 5. Koshōden. 6. Anpukuden. 7. Shunkōden.
8. Right guard. 9. Left guard. 10. Car house. 11. Empress Shinden.
12. Kitchens. Fig. 2. Plan of Shinden style mansion.

Plate 37

町 京 春
部

Streets in the capital of Heian.

Plate 38

Phoenix Hall (Hōō-do) of the Byōdōin at Uji. Plan, triple bracketing, hand-rail and pendant of gable.

Plate 39

Hall of the Fukiji temple in Bungo, Kyushu.   Elevation and section.

Plate 40

The Hakusui Amida-do, Uchigo village, Iwaki district, Fukushima province. Elevation and section. Built in 1160.

Plate 41

Reconstruction of the city of Hiraizumi after Sato. (A) Mansion of Yasuhira. (B) Mansion of Hidehira. (C) Great palace. (D) Ni-no-maru. (E) Willow palace. (F) Benkei's house. (G) Mansion of Takahira. (H) Mansion of Kunihira. (I) Chusonji temple. (J) Moetsuji. (K) Treasure house. (L) Gion shrine. (M) Sarusawa lake. (N) Nekoma lake. (O) Nobles' mansions. (P) Samurai residences.

Plate 42

The Konjikido of the Chusonji.

Plate 43

Five-story pagoda of the Daigōji. Crest of the stupa-pinnacle (Kurin).

Breadth of roofs (from lowest upwards):

feet	difference
21·7	
19·6	2·1
17·4	2·2
15·1	2·3
13·6½	2·4½

Height of roofs (from lowest upwards):

16·7	
30·1	13·4
42·7	12·6
55	12·3
66·8	11·8

Plate 44

119.4

41

78.4

68.8

11.8   X

52.2.

12.3

42.7.

12.6

30.1.

13.4   Y

16.7

Z

Five-storied pagoda of the Daigōji with geometrical proportions after the diagram of Professor Amanuma. Radius of circle X = ¼ of height of body of pagoda; radius of circle Y = ⅓ of height of body of pagoda; radius of circle Z = ½ of circle Y.

Plate 45

Fɪɢ. 1

Fɪɢ. 2

Fɪɢ. 1. The Hachiman shrine at Usa. Side and front views. Rebuilt in 1857. Edo period.
Fɪɢ. 2. The Hiyoshi shrine at Hieizan. Side view. Rebuilt in 1583. Momoyama period.

Plate 46

The Kamo shrine, Kyoto. Side and front views. Rebuilt in 1863. Edo period.

Plate 47

Professor Amanuma's restoration of the Yugi pagoda of Mount Koya.

Plate 48

Kamakura, with Shogun's mansion inset, after Sato

Shogun's mansion: (*a*) Tozamurai. (*b*) Shikidai. (*c*) Car approach. (*d*) Middle gate. (*e*) Great chamber. (*f*) Court nobles' chamber. (*g*) Chōdai. (*h*) Dais chamber. (*i*) Great corridor. (*j*) Audience chamber. (*k*) Bed chamber. (*l*) Tonomo. (*m*) Storeroom. (*n*) Common room. (*o*) Bathroom. (*p*) Hawks. (*q*) Stable. (*r*) Fodder. (*s*) Yagura gate. 1. Kenchoji. 2. Engakuji. 3. Sufukuji: 4. Jochiji. 5. Jomyoji (five Zen temples). 6. Great Buddha. 7. Hase Kwannon. 8. Gokurakuji. 9. Tsurugaoka Hachiman. 10. Kamakura station. 11. Yoritomo's mansion. 12. Wada's mansion. 13. Hatakeyama's mansion. 14. Saimyoji temple.

Plate 49

Mansion of the governor of the Eastern Provinces (Kanto-Kanryo) at Kamakura in the
Muromachi period.

Plate 50

産出の族貴代時倉鎌

A birth. Showing the interior of a mansion, Kamakura period.

Plate 51

鐮倉時代僧庵の書院

The Shōin of a monastery.

Plate 52

Fig. 1

Fig. 2

Fig. 1. Wall and gate with guard-house over it, in military residence of Kamakura period.
Fig. 2. Bell-tower of the Tōdaiji, Vara, side view elevation and section, front view half-section.

Plate 53

The three-story pagoda of the Kōfukuji, Nara. Early Kamakura style. Built
in 1141 by the Empress Taiken-monin.

Plate 54

Stupa-shaped pagoda (Tahoto) of Ishiyama temple. Built by Minamoto Yoritomo. This and another at the Kongo Sammai-in at Mount Koya are the oldest specimens of the kind. Height 55 feet, base 25 feet square. Shape the same as that of the Daito, but smaller. Dimensions of Daito 150 feet high, base 140 feet square.

Plate 55

FIG. 1

FIG. 2

FIG. 3

The Nandaimon of the Tōdaiji. FIG. 1. Front elevation. FIG. 2. Side section. FIG. 3. Enlarged detail of the seven branch bracketing.

Plate 56

Fig. 1

Fig. 2

Fig. 3

Fig. 4

Fig. 5

Details of the Kanshinji. Fig. 1. Lobster tie-beam (*ebi Koryo*). Fig. 2. Beam-end (*keta-kakushi*). Fig. 3. Ornamental finial (*tabasami*). Fig. 4. King-post (*heisoku*). Fig. 5. Verge board (*gegyo*).

Plate 57

Fig. 1

Fig. 2

FIG. 1. The Shariden of the Engakuji, Kamakura.
FIG. 2. Details of the Engakuji Shariden. 1. Tie-
beam. 2. Mortised bracket (*sashi-hijiki*).
3. Great capital. 4. Plate. 5. Pillar brace.
6. Tail rafter brackets (*tabasami*). 7. Upper tie-
beam. 8. Lobster tie-beam.

Plate 58

F<small>IG</small>. 1

F<small>IG</small>. 2

F<small>IG</small>. 1. Renge gate of the Toji Temple, Kyoto. Repaired by Minamoto Yoritomo in 1199, at the request of Mongaku Shonin. F<small>IG</small>. 2. Details of roof construction of the Kamakura period. Kozanji temple, Chofu, Yamaguchi prefecture. 1. Tie-beam (*koryo*). 2. Great king-post (*o-heisoku*). 3. Pillar brace (*to-nuki*). 4. Plate (*dairin*). 5. Brace nosing (*to-nuki-bana*). 6. Lobster tie-beam (*ebi Koryo*). 7. Tail rafter (*o-daruki*).

Plate 59

Fɪɢ. 1

Fɪɢ. 2

The Sutra library (Kyozo) at Kami Daigo temple.   Fɪɢ. 1. Front view section.
Fɪɢ. 2. Side view section.

Plate 60

Fig. 1

Fig. 2

FIG. 1. Kanshinji temple, side view. FIG. 2. The Kaisando or Founder's Hall of the Eihōji.
Toyooka village, Gefu prefecture.   Built in 1352.   Kamakura period.

Plate 61

The octagonal pagoda of the Anrakuji temple at Bessho village, Chiisagata
district, province of Nagano.

Plate 62

0   10   20   30   40   50   60   70   80

The Great Pagoda (Daito) of Negoro temple.   Elevation and section.

Plate 63

Ginkakuji, Kyoto. Front view and side view.

Plate 64

Fig. 1

Fig. 2

Fig. 3

Fig. 4

Fig. 5

Fig. 6

Details of the Kinkakuji. Fig. 1. Balcony. Fig. 2. Foliate window. Fig. 3. Double leaf door. Fig. 4. Gable pendant. Fig. 5. Balcony rail. Fig. 6. King-post.

Plate 65

Fɪɢ. 1

Fɪɢ. 2

Fɪɢ. 3

Fɪɢ. 9

Fɪɢ. 4

Fɪɢ. 5

Fɪɢ. 6

Fɪɢ. 7

Fɪɢ. 8

Fɪɢ. 10

Fɪɢ. 1. Side view of the Ki-bitsu shrine, Ichinomiya, Okayama prefecture; built in 1390.
Fɪɢs 2 to 10. Decorated beam-ends from the bell-tower of the Tōdaiji, Nara. Fɪɢs 2 to 8
Kamakura period. Fɪɢs 9 and 10. Muromachi period.

Plate 66

FIG. 1

FIG. 2

FIG. 1. Oshi-ita. FIG. 2. Early form of *shōji*, called
Konmeichi *shōji*. The modern *tsuitate* or single-leaf
screen.

Plate 67

LAKE

BIWA

MARSH

TO HACHIMAN

TO HIKONE

Azuchi castle. 1. Gate of Sōgenji. 2. Three-storied pagoda. 3. Main temple of Sōgenji. 4. Guest house. 5. Kitchen and refectory. 6. Oda Nobutada's mansion. 7. Takei Sekian's mansion. 8. Toyotomi Hideyoshi's mansion. 9. Tokugawa Ieyasu's mansion. 10. Muto Sukeemon's mansion. 11. Eto Kagaemon's mansion. 12. Chujo Shogen's mansion. 13. Tearooms. 14. Hasegawa mansion. 15. Oda Nobuzumi's mansion. 16. Ichibashi Shimosa's mansion. 17. Sugaya Kyuemon's mansion. 18. Hori Kyutaro's mansion. 19. Iron Gate. 20. Outer ward (Ni-no-maru). 21. Inner ward (Hon Maru). 22. Outer terrace. 23. Upper terrace of Hon Maru. 24. Keep (Tenshu). 25. Steps from Sōgenji. 26 Main approach from highway.

Plate 68

FIG. 1

FIG. 2

FIG. 3

FIG. 4

FIG. 5

FIG. 1. Plan of Osaka castle, as the fortress of the Hongwanji monks, and as reconstructed by Hideyoshi.   FIG. 2. Old sketch of fortified field head-quarters about 1600.   FIG. 3. Rampart of Osaka castle.   FIG. 4. Gate of the castle of Sakura.   FIG. 5. Castle Gate (Masugata).

Plate 69

TEN MA.R

YODO·R.

IMAFUKU

SHIGINO

NEKOMA·R.

HIRANO·R.

Keep

Hon Maru

Ni·ho·Maru

Sanada Maru

Okayama

Chausuyama

Osaka castle as defended by Hideyori in 1614.

Plate 70

FIG. 1

FIG. 2

FIG. 1. Kitchen and refectory of the Myōhōin, Kyoto; side view and front view.
FIG. 2. The eight-fold roof of the Momoyama period. The most complicated type of shrine roof.

Plate 71

Dai-butsu-den or hall of the Great Buddha of the Tōdaiji, Nara.

Plate 72

FIG. 1

FIG. 2

FIG. 1. The Great Buddha temple of the Hōkōji from a picture of 1794. FIG. 2. The Hiunkaku of the Nishi Hongwanji from the western side.

Plate 73

Fig. 1

Fig. 2

Fig. 3

Fig. 4

The Kokakudai bathroom of the Hiunkaku. Fig. 1. Front view. Fig. 2. Section of front view.
Fig. 3. Section through side of centre. Fig. 4. Section through bath chamber.

Plate 74

Fɪɢ. 1

Fɪɢ. 2

Fɪɢ. 3

The Hiunkaku villa.   Fɪɢ. 1. Front view.   Fɪɢ. 2. Plan of ground, first and second floors.
Fɪɢ. 3. Side view from the west.

Plate 75

Jinya or official residence of a smaller feudal lord or local official. The Nagaya or
"long-house" is the lodging of the retainers and the Kura a fireproof store-house.

Plate 76

The castle and town of Fukuoka, built and laid out by Kuroda Josui and his son Nagamasa after 1600. (S) Samurai. (T) Townsmen. Fukuoka lies on the sea which is utilized to form the moats. The quarter of the traders lies in the centre on the main street with that of the artisans in the rear.

Plate 77

Plan of the Hon-maru of the Castle of Fukuoka, built by Kuroda Josui and his son Nagamasa, 1603-1610. (a) Entrance hall, 32 mats. (b) Inner hall, 24 mats. (c) Great chamber, 56 mats. (d) Plum chamber, 10 mats. (e) Bamboo chamber. (f) Long alcove chamber, 28 mats. (g) Palanquin chamber, 8 mats. (h) Chamber of the gentlemen-in-waiting. (i) Chamber of the steward of the household. (j) Waiting-room, 8 mats. (k) Living-room. (l) Bed-chamber. (m) Chamber of the hearth. (n) Dark chamber. (o) Kitchen. (p) Utensil pantry. (q) Lantern room, 8 mats. (r) Small chamber. (s) Corridor. (t) Sitting-room, 8 mats. (u) Dais. (v) Armour room, 18 mats. (w) Guard-room. (x) Courtyards. (y) Privy. (z) Fire buckets. 1 Alcove. 2 Cupboards. 3 Veranda.

Plate **78**

LAKE

SHINJI.

Plan of the castle town of Matsue, Province of Izumo, one of the "water capitals" of Japan. Here again the residences of the greater Samurai are round the castle (A) and those of the middle class on the outskirts of the town (B) while the trading quarter is across the Ohashi bridge, along Shirakata Machi and Tenjin Machi, continuing along Suetsugu Hon Machi by the lakeside. Beyond this across the Tenjin river lies the quarter of the smaller Samurai or Ashigaru in Saiga Machi (C) The temples are all massed in Tera Machi behind the trading quarter except a few that lie at the foot of the hills. Few cities in Japan are more charmingly situated.

FIG. 1. Plan of the Hon Maru of Okayama castle. 1. Keep. 2. Salt storehouse. 3. Oil storehouse. 4. Treasuries. 5. Arsenals. 6. Rice storehouse. 7. Towers. 8. Tamon. 9. Gates.
FIG. 2. The mansion of the Hon Maru of Okayama castle in the time of Ikeda Mitsumasa, 1632-1672. From Ikeda Mitsumasa Kō Den. 1. Entrance. 2. Entrance porch. 3. Corridor. 4. Guard-room. 5. Bodyguard room (6).* 6. Envoys' room (8). 7. Foot-soldiers' guard-room (30). 8. Common room (8). 9. Plum chamber (36). 10. Bamboo chamber (18). 11. Eaves chamber (23). 12. Fir chamber (20). 13. South inner corridor (10). 14. South inner corridor (6). 15. Deer chamber (31). 16. Ante-chamber (10). 17. Wistaria chamber (15). 18. Pine chamber, with Toko (12½). 19. Plover chamber (15). 20. Perching bird chamber (15). 21. Panelled chamber (15). 22. Descending step chamber (18). 23. Papered chamber (15). 24. Back porch. 25. Guard-room (7). 26. Spear chamber (30). 27. Sheaved straw chamber, with Toko (16). 28. Seal-shaped chamber (8). 29. Small common room (12). 30. Board-floor kitchen. 31. Kitchen (22). 32. Kitchen (9). 33. Utensil pantry (11). 34. Liquor room (7). 35. Long hearth room (37). 36. Middle inner common room (7). 37. Deputy's room (6). 38. Middle chamber, upper (9). 39. Middle chamber, ante-chamber (17½). 40. Middle chamber, third chamber (10). 41. Resting chamber (10). 42. Corridor (11). 43. Footguard captains' common room (20). 44. Passage chamber (21). 45. Servery (6). 46. Bow chamber (22½). 47. Ceremonial tea-room (4½). 48. Ceremonial ante-chamber with three-mat Mizuya (6). 49. Secretary's room (10). 50. Bodyguard's common room (6). 51. Pages' room (5½). 52. Tea-room (4). 53. Clock chamber (6). 54. Cloud beckoning pavilion: Upper chamber, with dais, Toko and shelves in L-shaped section of four mats (13). 55. Cloud beckoning pavilion: south chamber (12). 56. Cloud beckoning pavilion: second chamber (12). 57. Cloud beckoning pavilion: third chamber (18). 58. Fan chamber (10). 59. Mirror chamber (12). 60. Dais chamber. (4½). 61. Corridor leading to Sukigata tower (14). 62. South parlour: upper chamber (10). 63. South parlour: second chamber (16). 64. South parlour: third chamber (5). 65. New parlour (8). 66. New parlour: ante-chamber (7½). 67. Corridor.

* Figures refer to number of mats.

Plate 79

FIG. 1

FIG. 2

Plate 80

Plan of the castle town of Okayama. The streets of the tradesmen are in the centre of the city in Kami-no-cho, Naka-no-cho to Sakae-cho, and along Saidaiji-cho, the main thoroughfare across the bridge. They lie between the quarters of the great vassals (A) and those of middle class (B). The artisans are situated farther out in Togiya-cho and Daiku-cho, while the lesser retainers (C) live in Bancho. (卍 Temple. 卅 Shrine.)

Plate 81

FIG. 1

FIG. 2

FIG. 1. Plan of the moated castle town of Okayama, Bizen. FIG. 2. Plan of the Clan College (Han Gakko) at Okayama, now used as the normal school of the prefecture. 1. Gate and guard-house. 2. Pond and bridge. 3, 4. Left and right classrooms. 5, 6. Left and right stairs. 7. Great hall. 8. Middle hall. 9. Dining-hall. 10-14. Cryptomeria, Sophora, willow, bamboo and pine lodgings. 15-19. Paulownia, orange, plum, orchid and chryanthemum lodgings. 20. Shooting range. 21. Library. 22. Kitchen. 23. Back gate. 24. Bath house. 25. Official quarters. 26. Servants' quarters. 27. Rice store.

Plate 82

Plan of the castle town of Takada in Echigo, showing the quarters of the Samurai round the castle and those of the tradesmen and artisans along the main road. T. Townsmen.

Plate 83

Nagasaki Bay

Plan of the city of Nagasaki. Nagasaki was a purely mercantile port in charge of the central government under a commissioner. There was no castle and no Samurai quarter. The streets are named from the various trades carried on in them, or after other towns from which their inhabitants originally came when the city grew in the late sixteenth century from a small fishing village to a big town as the result of trade with Europe. Its temples and shrines are all arranged at the foot of the hills that rise behind it.

Several of them are built on the sites of former Catholic churches.

Plate 84

FIG. 1

FIG. 2

FIG. 1. Keep of the castle of Nagoya. FIG. 2. Keep of Matsue; five stories, six floors; 1600.

Plate 85

FIG. 1

FIG. 2

FIG. 3

FIG. 4

FIG. 1. Keep of Okayama castle; five stories, six floors; 1597. FIG. 2. Keep of Inuyama castle; four stories, five floors; 1600. FIG. 3. Keep of Kumamoto castle; double towers; 1596. Okayama castle keep is said to have been built on the model of that of Nobunaga at Azuchi and to resemble it exteriorly though its interior is quite as bare as the rest. FIG. 4. The keep of the castle of Matsumoto in Shinano; five stories, six floors; 1590.

Plate 86

Fig. 1

Fig. 2

Fig. 1. The original keep of Edo castle from an old picture. Fig. 2. Flanking guard-house at entrance of Edo castle.

Plate 87

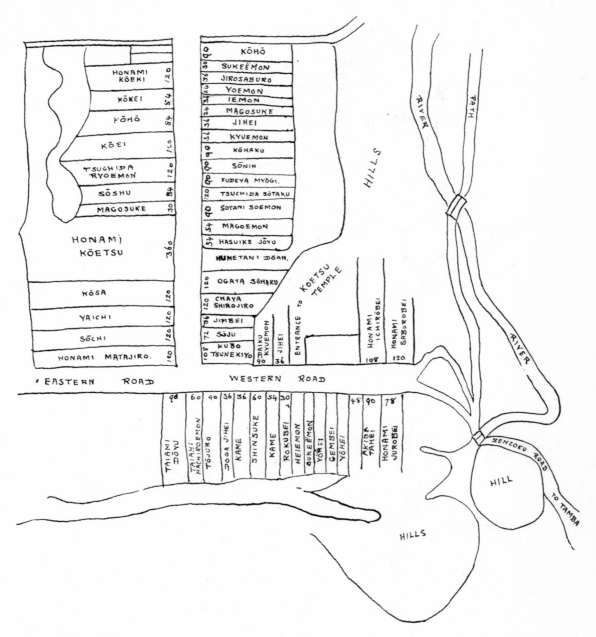

Village of craftsmen laid out by Honami Kōetsu at Takagamine near Kyoto. Early seventeenth century.

Plate 88

Edo castle.　General plan.

Plate 89

EDO CASTLE.

O Omote or Outer Palace
of the Hon Maru.

Ō·ŌKU

NAKA·ŌKU

Ō·OMOTE

Edo castle. O Omote or Outer Palace of the Hon Maru. 1. Minor construction office. 2. Chief page. 3. Surgeon. 4. Secretary. 5. Pages of the interior. 6. Pages. 7. Minor ten men guard. 8. Present guard. 9. Shogun's private guard. 10. Commissioner for works. 11. Commissioner for timber. 12. Investigators. 13. Ten men guard control. 14. Chief of the Shōin guard. 15. Envoys. 16. Chief of Oban guard. 17. O Tsukai guard. 18. Secretary. 19. New guard. 20. Middle interior guard. 21. Soshaban chamberlains. 22. Temple and shrine commissioner. 23. Master of ceremonies. 24. City commissioner. 25. Captain of the new guard. 26. Metsuke. 27. Commissioner for works. 28. Commissioner for buildings. 29. Commissioner for minor repairs. 30. Captain of the corps of pages. 31. Finance commissioner. 32. Metsuke. 33. Bird room. 34. Garden's room. 35. Chief Bozu of the interior. 36. Overseer of small gear. 37. Bozu pages of the interior. 38. Ablution room. 39. Chiefs' room. 40. Store-room. 41. Conversation room. 42. Carpenters' room. 43. Cooks. 44. Six-mat room. 45. Bedclothes room. 46. Chamberlains' rest room. 47. Chamberlains' conversation room. 48. Two-story Nando.

Plate 90

Edo castle. O Oku or Inner Palace of the Hon Maru, plan 1. 1. Dais chamber. 2. Lower dais. 3. Ante-chamber. 4. Third chamber. 5. Sitting-room. 6. Living-room. 7. Bed chamber. 8. Dressing chamber. 9. Secretary's room. 10. Guest chamber. 11. Tea-room. 12. Kettle room. 13. Cake room. 14. Store-room. 15. Kitchen. 16. Pantry. 17. Scullery. 18. Oil room. 19. Messengers' room. 20. Lady councillors' room. 21. Cooling pavilion. 22. Earthquake refuge. 23. Bathroom. 24. Common room. 25. Tamari. 26. Liquor room. 27. Costumiers' room. 28. O Kiyo costumiers' room. 29. Upper Tsubone. 30. Lower Tsubone. 31. Seat. 32. Gate. 33. Irikawa. 34. Corridor. 35. Guard-room. 36. Maids' room. 37. Maids' corridor. 38. Lantern room. 39. Copper jar room. 40. Ladies' apartment. 41. Earth-floored space. 42. Charcoal store. 43. Iga guard common room. 44. Iga guard quarters. 45. Men's room. 46. Hireling's room. 47. Palanquin house. 48. Firewood store. 49. Tower guard quarters. 50. Present room. 51. Key-guard room. 52. Permit room.

Plate 91

Edo castle. O Oku or Inner Palace of the Hon Maru, plan 2.

Plan of the mansion of a court noble built in 1713 in Imadegawa Street, Kyoto, for Lord Nijo Yoshitada, son of Lord Nijo Tsunahira, Minister of the Right, by Maeda Tsunatoshi, Lord of Kaga, whose daughter the Lady Eiko married Yoshitada. This alliance between the daughter of the wealthiest Daimyo and the son of one of the five regent families of the Court nobility was arranged by the Lady Keishoin, mother of the Shogun Tokugawa Tsunayoshi.

Front court and reception rooms. 1. Front gate. 2. Guard-house. 3. Samurai waiting-room. 4. Palanquin house. 5. Library. 6. Outer porch (Shiki-dai). 7. Guard-room. 8. Great reception chamber. 9. Envoys' chamber. 10. Rest room for guards of the great chamber. 11. Guest room. 11a. Senior lady attendants' room (Joshu-toshiyori-bansho). 11b. Girl attendants' room (Hanjo-beya). 11c. Between maids' room (Nakai-beya). Private living-rooms. 12. Vestibule (Yori-tsuki). 13. Ante-room (O-tsugi). 14. Sitting-room (O-cha-no-ma). 15. Living-room (O-Ima). 16. Dais sitting-room (Goza-no-ma, Go-Jodan). 17. Dressing-room. 18. Bed chamber. 19. Birth chamber. 20. Wardrobe chamber (O Nando). 21. Bathroom. 22. Toilet room. 23. Sewing room with lookout above. 24. Store for wine and confectionary. 25. Lamp and candle room. 26. Councillors' office (Toshiyori Yakusho). 27. Chamber of the ladies-in-waiting (Tsubone Goyo-no-ma). 28. Wardrobe storehouse. Observation chambers. 29. Two sitting-rooms with ante-rooms looking out on the Imadegawa street front and connected with the private apartments by a corridor. Detached quarters for the old people and children. 30. Veranda sitting-room (Go En-zashiki). 31. School-room. 32. Wardrobe room. 33. Dressing-room. 34. Bathroom. 35. Tutor's room. 36. Instruction room. 37. Wet nurses' room. 38. Old people's room. 39. Women's room. 40. Maids' room. Four sets of apartments for ladies-in-waiting, each flat consisting of: 41. Living-room. 42. Storeroom. 43. Ante-room. 44. Kitchen and privy. Two blocks containing twelve sets for the maids (Jōchu), each consisting of two rooms of equal size in seven flats and with a larger living-room in five, two guest rooms, two small bathrooms attached to the guest rooms, and one large common bathroom for the maids. 45. Living-room. 46. Ante-room. 47. Earth-floored kitchen. 48. Bathroom. 49. Maid servants' common bathroom. 50 Dressing-room. A block consisting of one larger residence with a stable and six smaller ones, for male officials. The small flats consist of two with: 51. Living-room. 52. Ante-room. 53. Chamber. 54. Storeroom. 55. Earth-floored kitchen, and four with the same arrangement but lacking the ante-room. The larger residence contains: 56. Entrance hall. 57. Reception room. 58. Ante-room. 59. Living-room. 60. Storeroom. 61. Kitchen. 62. Stable. Kitchen block. 63. Servery. 64. Pantry for utensils, cakes and *sake* (two-story). 65. Family dining-room (Go-zensho). 66. Kitchen for vegetarian food (Go-seisho). 67. Great kitchen. 68. Waiting-room (Tamari-no-ma), two-story. 69. Chef's room (two-story). 70. Waiting-room for officers of the vegetarian kitchen (two-story). 71. Earth-floored vestibule. 72. Back entrance. 73. Outer porch of back entrance. 74. Guard-rooms. 75. Waiting-room for officials. 76. Rest room. 77. Inner rest room. 78. Storeroom. 79. Fuel room. 80. Middle gate. 81. Guard-room. 82. Guards' rest room. 83. Craftsmen's workshop. 84. Kitchen storeroom. 85. Rice room. 86. Storehouse for rice. 87. Storehouse for salt, *miso, sake* and other culinary articles. 88. Storeroom. 89. Outer rest room. 90. Back gate. 91. Outer porch. 92. Guard-room. 93. Guards' rest room. 94. Maids' palanquin house. 95. Bearers. 96. Under servants. (a) Wall. (b) Postern. (c) Court. (d) Well. (e) Corridor. (f) Tally office (Kitte Bansho). (g) Bath furnace room. (h) Fence. (x) Privy.

Plate 92

Imadegawa Street.

Plate 93

Gates of Diamyos' mansions in Edo. FIG. 1. Lord of a province, highest grade. FIG. 2. Lord of a province, second grade. FIG. 3. Lords above 100,000 *koku*. FIG. 4. Lords over 50,000 *koku*. FIG. 5. Lords from 10,000 to 50,000 *koku*. FIG. 6. Tozama lords and branch houses of lords of provinces above and below 50,000 *koku*. FIGS 7 and 8. Gate of lord of highest grade as rebuilt after a fire.

Plate 94

Fɪɢ. 1

Fɪɢ. 2

Fɪɢ. 1. Plan of the Tōshōgu shrine at Nikko. (*a*) Front gate. (*b*) Five-storied pagoda. (*c*) Stable. (*d*) Water basin. (*e*) Library. (*f*) Lower treasury. (*g*) Middle treasury. (*h*) Upper treasury. (*i*) Privy (Seijo). (*j*) Drum tower. (*k*) Bell-tower. (*l*) Yakushi hall. (*m*) Shrine office. (*n*) Yomei-mon. (*o*) Car house. (*p*) Kagura stage. (*q*) Upper shrine office. (*r*) Kara-mon. (*s*) Oratory. (*t*) Stone chamber. (*u*) Main shrine. (*v*) Cloister. (*w*) Saka-no-shita gate. (*x*) Oratory. (*y*) Bronze gate. (*z*) Stupa tomb. Fɪɢ. 2. Plan of Nijo castle. 1. Entrance. 2. Tōzamurai. 3. O-biroma (great reception chamber). 4. Kuro Shōin (black reception chamber). 5 Shiro Shōin (white reception chamber).

Plate 95

Upper section of the five-storied pagoda at Nikko.

Plate 96

Lower section of the five-storied pagoda at Nikko.

Plate 97

Fig. 2

Fig. 1. Plan of the Zen temple of Myōshinji, Kyoto. 1. Envoy's gate. 2. Main gate. 3. Pond. 4. Sammon. 5. Buddha hall. 6. Hatto. 7. Shindo. 8. Great residence. 9. Small residence. 10. Great corridor. 11. Kitchen and refectory. 12. Library. 13. Belfry. 14. Bath house.

Fig. 2. Plan of the kitchen and refectory of the Myōshinji, built in 1654. (a) Entrance hall. (b) Great kitchen. (c) Small kitchen. (d) Refectory. (e) Buddha shrine. (f) Council chamber. (g) Provost's office. (h) Great corridor. (i) Passage to residence.

Fig. 1

Plate 98

Zen temple of Manpukuji. 1. Main gate. 2. Sammon. 3. Tenno-
den. 4. Moon terrace. 5. Buddha hall. 6. Hatto. 7. Itoku-den.
8. Western residence. 9. Eastern residence. 10. Shrine hall. 11. Meditation hall. 12. Seido. 13. Refectory and kitchen. 14. Ancestors'
hall. 15. Garando. 16. Drum tower. 17. Bell-tower. 18. Hall of
lights. 19. Founder's hall. 20. Residence.

Plate 99

Imperial Palace, Kyoto. Kōka gate and Seiryōden.

Plate 100

Imperial Palace, Kyoto. Front gate and Shishinden.

Plate 101

The Imperial Palace shrine or Kashiko-dokoro (Place of Awe). In the centre is the Kashiko-dokoro itself where the Sun-Goddess is enshrined. On the left is the Kōrei-den or Imperial Ancestral Spirit Hall, where the spirits of the Former Emperors are revered, and on the right the Shinden or Hall of the Deities dedicated to other important deities of the country. The tiled structure on the left is the Ablution Place, while the other buildings before the front gate and to the right are the Kagura and Hōraku stages for the sacred music and dance.

Plate 102

FIG. 1. Front of a theatre. 1. Entrance to stalls. 2. Other entrances. 3. Ticket office. 4. Seat. 5. Drum tower.
FIG. 2. The theatre quarter of Saru-waka-cho. (*x*) Bath house. (*y*) First-class tea-house. (*z*) Second- and third-class tea-house. (*o*) Actors' residences.

Plate 103

Plan of the Yoshiwara pleasure quarter in Edo, showing the great gate and
street gates. The names of the principal houses are given.

Plate 104

Fig. 1

Fig. 2

Fig. 3

FIG. 1. Side street in Edo with guard-house and gates for closing the thoroughfare.
FIG. 2. Fireman's watch-tower. Street fire-buckets beneath. FIG. 3. Fire-proof storehouse.

Plate 105

FIG. 1

FIG. 1. Plan of public bath house with two baths, at Osaka. (*a*) Bath tubs. (*b*) Seats. (*c*) Hot rinsing water tank. (*d*) Cold water tank. (*e*) Washing place (stone floor). (*f*) Pay desk. (*g*) Clothes locker. (*h*) Undressing room (board floor). (*i*) Entry (earth floor). (*j*) Outer door.

FIG. 2. Plan of public bath house in Edo. (*a*) Well. (*b*) Cold water tank. (*c*) Men's bath. (*d*) Women's bath. (*e*) Hot rinsing water tank. (*f*) Washing place (stone floor). (*g*) Cold water tank. (*h*) Gutter. (*i*) Board partition. (*j*) Undressing room (board floor). (*k*) Clothes lockers. (*l*) Entry (earth floor). (*m*) Pay desk. (*n*) Outer door. (*o*) Clothes lockers with lattice window over. This represents the type of public bath house in use after 1830 when the government ordered separate compartments to be made for men and women, and a wooden partition about shoulder high was then put down the middle.

FIG. 3. Bath tub with gabled porch in public bath house.

FIG. 2

FIG. 3

Plate 106

Bathroom interior. (After a print by Torii Kiyonaga.)

Plate 107

FIG. 1

FIG. 1. Large farm-house in Tsutsuki village, Kyoto. (*a*) Entrance. (*b*) Middle chamber. (*c*) Kitchen. (*d*) Buddhist shrine chamber. (*e*) Reception room. (*f*) Chamber. (*g*) Inner chamber. (*h*) Bridge. (*i*) Detached rooms for retired members. (*j*) Storehouses. (*k*) Barn. (*l*) Sitting-rooms. (*m*) Earth-floored space. (*n*) Outhouse. (*o*) Garden. (*p*) Pond. (*q*) Bridge. (*r*) Moat. (*s*) Manservant's room. (*t*) Storeroom. (*u*) Well. (*v*) Stove. (*x*) Privy. (*y*) Court. (*z*) Bathroom.

FIG. 2. Narrow residence characteristic of Kyoto, known as "eel housing". (*a*) Entry. (*b*) Vestibule. (*c*) Kitchen. (*d*) Living-room. (*e*) Court. (*f*) Store house. (*g*) Sink. (*h*) Scullery. (*i*) Cupboards. (*j*) Store. (*k*) Lattice window.

FIG. 2

Plate 108

Korean peasant's house built of logs and mud, with heating system under the floor and warm chamber. This closed style of dwelling is more like the Japanese Nando or Kura than anything else in that country.

Plate 109.

Kachu-yashiki or Samurai residence at Kita-bori, Matsue. This is the house that was occupied by Lafcadio Hearn and described in his *Glimpses of Unfamiliar Japan,* vol. ii, Chap. I. It is now preserved as a memorial to him.

Plate 110

Garden

12.

4½   6

Covered Way   Kura

Cu Cupb Toko

Receplin Room 10

10

Garden

8   8

Bath

6

Stove Earth floor

6   Entry 3   3

8

Garden.

Porch

Count

Kura   8   Gate House   entry   8

look-out   3

Street

Side Street.

FIG. 1

FIG. 2

FIG. 1. Plan of the residence of a Samurai of middle class. FIG. 2. Street front and gatehouse of above.

Plate 111

A Benie print-seller. He carried a pack on his back the upper part of which is a model of the Miuraya brothel, the name of which is visible on the *noren* or hanging curtain. On the side of the house are the characters for Yoshiwara and a little below a flag inscribed Great Gate Entrance. Below this again is written "Elegant red coloured and lacquered pictures". The buckets at the side and the tub on the roof are precautions against fire.
Date: the era Kyoho (1716-1736).

Plate 112

Fig. 1

Fig. 2

Fig. 1. Privy of an inn at the end of a short covered way at right angles to a veranda. Tastefully constructed of natural wood. Fig. 2. The interior with ventilation window. (After Morse.)

Plate 113

Tiles. 1, 2. Flat tiles. 3, 4. Eave tiles. 5, 6. Ridge tiles. 7, 8, 9. Pan tiles. 10. Jointed tiles, for wall tops. 11. Valley tiles. 12. Flat vine-pattern tiles. 13. Pantile vine-pattern tiles. 14. Corner vine-pattern tiles. 15, 16. Round cover tiles. Antefix tiles. 18. Demon-face tile and base. 19, 20, 21. Demon plate finials. 22. Pantiles, with wind-break (*a*) and eave tiles (*b*). 23. Hip ridge built up with ridge tiles. 24. Gable end with eave tiles and demon plate finial. 25. Ridge tile with acroterion (*a*). 26. Side view of same. 27. Ditto, another pattern. 28. Ditto, built up with linked round tiles. 29. Hip ridge with supernumerary finial. 30. Tiles bedded on clay and nailed. 31. Hip ridge with demon plate. 32. Linked round tiles. 33. Flat tiles with round cover and antefix tiles. 34. Method of laying pantiles.

Plate 114

Roof shapes. Fɪɢ. 1. Gable (Kiritsuma). Fɪɢ. 2. Hip (Azumaya). Fɪɢ. 3. Hipped gable (Irimoya). Fɪɢ. 4. Single end hipped gable (Kata Irimoya). Fɪɢ. 5. Hip with lean-to (Hisashi Azumaya). Fɪɢ. 6. Pyramidal roof (Hōkei). Fɪɢ. 7. Neck-guard style hipped gable (Shikoro Irimoya). Fɪɢ. 8. Chinese gable (Kara Hafu). Fɪɢ. 9. Chinese and ordinary gable (Kiritsuma Karahafu). Fɪɢ. 10. One wing style (Tsunoya). Fɪɢ. 11. Double wing style (Kagiya or Kudo-tsukuri, key-shape or stove-shape).

Plate 115

Lattice windows.

Plate 116

Staircases.

Plate 117

Fig. 1

Fig. 2

Fig. 3

Fig. 4

Fig. 5

Fig. 6

Ceilings.   Fig. 1. Ordinary or *sao-buchi* ceiling.   Fig. 2. Construction of ordinary ceiling from above.   Fig. 3. Coffered ceiling.   Fig. 4. Coffered cove ceiling.   Fig. 5. Ogee curved ceiling.   Fig. 6. Coffered ceiling and dressed rafter roof.

Plate 118

Fig. 1

Fig. 2

Fig. 3

Fig. 4

Fig. 5   Fig. 6   Fig. 7

Wooden lanterns. Their inscriptions advertise: Fig. 1. Oil. Fig. 2. Bean paste. Fig. 3. Spaghetti. Fig. 4. Paste. Fig. 5. Vermicelli.
Fig. 6. Restaurant lantern. Fig. 7. Roofed water basin.

Plate 119

Hot spring bath houses.

Plate 120

F<small>IG</small>. 1

F<small>IG</small>. 2

F<small>IG</small>. 1. The simple staircase of an inn. F<small>IG</small>. 2. A renaissance cupola added to a hot spring
bathing hotel in pure Japanese style.

Plate 121

Plan and elevation of a modern house in Japanese style. Area of ground floor, 38 *tsubo** 2·5. Area of upper floor, 11 *tsubo* 5. Total area, 49 *tsubo* 7·5. Timber, cryptomeria and pine. Mats and tategu, i.e. *shōji, fusuma* and doors of medium class. Price in yen: ground floor, 5737·50; upper floor, 1725; total 7462·50; average cost per *tsubo* 150 (£15).

Here the family block for the wife and servant and children is by itself to the right of the entrance with a room for the Shosei or student page by the vestibule. Two living-rooms lead directly from the vestibule, and the reception or guest room is beyond it. Upstairs are two rooms similar in size to those below them.

* A *tsubo* equals 2 mats, or 6 x 6 feet.

Plate 122

Section of an ordinary Japanese house to show construction. Also detail of dovetailing of corner of beams and pillar base, and of corner roof beams.